Francis W. Newman

Contributions chiefly to the early History of the late Cardinal Newman

Francis W. Newman

Contributions chiefly to the early History of the late Cardinal Newman

ISBN/EAN: 9783337061616

Printed in Europe, USA, Canada, Australia, Japan

Cover: Foto ©ninafisch / pixelio.de

More available books at **www.hansebooks.com**

CONTRIBUTIONS CHIEFLY TO THE EARLY HISTORY OF THE LATE CARDINAL NEWMAN.

WITH COMMENTS

BY HIS BROTHER,

F. W. NEWMAN,

Emeritus Professor of University College, London, etc., M.R.A.S.

LONDON:
KEGAN PAUL, TRENCH, TRÜBNER & Co., Ltd.
1891.

CONTENTS.

—:o:—

INTRODUCTION		v
CHAPTER I. EARLIEST TIMES BEFORE THE ORDINATION OF J. H. NEWMAN TO BE DEACON, 1824		1
„ II. EARLY PREACHING, UP TO 1832 ..		16
„ III. HIS HIGHEST ADVANCE AND SCHEMES. THE HAMPDEN BUBBLE		50
„ IV. DECLINE AND FALL		89
„ V. CONTRAST OF TWO CARDINALS. THE "APOLOGIA"		109
„ VI. RESPECTFUL ADDRESS TO ENGLISH PROTESTANTS		122

INTRODUCTION.

―:o:―

WHEN I began to write, it was with a different title, " Anti-Sacerdotalism," and with a difference of purpose which altered all my proportions. Further considerations and the urgency of friends induced a change.

No one living knows my brother's life from boyhood to the age of forty as I do. The splendour of his funeral makes certain that his early life will be written; it must be expected that the more *mythical* the narrative the better it will sell. The honour naturally and rightfully paid to him by Catholics makes him a public man of the century. I should have vastly preferred entire oblivion of him and his writings of the first forty years, but that is impossible. In the cause of *Protestants* and *Protestantism* I feel bound to write, however painful to myself, as simply as if my topic were an old Greek or Latin.

In my rising manhood I received inestimable benefits from this (my eldest) brother. I was able to repay his money, but that could not cancel my debt, for he supported me not out of his abundance, but when he knew not whence weekly and daily funds were to come. I have felt grateful up to his last day, and have tried to cherish for him a sort of *filial* sentiment. Yet a most painful breach, through mere religious creed, broke on me in my nineteenth year, and was *unhealable*. Each wished to the other everything best, yet the Church was to him everything, while the Church (as viewed by him from the day of his ordination) was to me NOTHING. Hence we seemed never to have an interest nor a wish in common.

That I have in my deepest aversion to Romanism no bigotry against Romanists, I am inwardly conscious by my warm honour and esteem for that thorough "*Papist*," Cardinal Manning. Wherever the doctrine of Rome clashes with Universal Protestantism, I account the Roman doctrine not un-Christian only, but barbaric and *Pagan*. But this does not make me forget that Romanism contains a vast mass of *that* doctrine which chiefly makes Christian sentiment valuable, and that the Church in its worst age had saints, before whom it were wholesome to bow, not because of their Creed, but because of their fundamental goodness.

I could not possibly have written freely of the late Cardinal to grieve him while he lived, but I see a new side of duty opened to me, now that my words cannot pain him.

It has of late been frequently said there were three Newmans, not two; and I had to defend the Cardinal once against the wholly unjust charge of neglecting my *second* brother, Charles Robert, whose wasted life were better buried in silence. But now I see that, unless *something* be explained by me, no one will guess at his very eccentric character, and false ideas are likely to gain currency.

In opening life, my brother C. R. N. became a convert to Robert Owen, the philanthropic

Socialist, who was *then* an Atheist. But soon breaking loose from him, Charles tried to originate a "New Moral World" of his own, which seemed to others absurd and immoral, as well as very unamiable. He disowned us all, on my father's death, as "too religious" for him. To keep a friend, or to act under a superior, seemed alike impossible to him. His brother (the late Cardinal) humbled himself to beg a clerkship for him in the Bank of England; but Charles thought it "his duty" to write to the Directors letters of advice, so they could not keep him. Nor could he keep any place long. He said he ought to take a literary degree at Bonn: his two brothers managed it for him, but he came away *without* seeking the degree. His brother-in-law (Rev. Th. Mozley) then took him up very liberally; but after my sister Harriet's death, J. H. N. and I bore his expenses to his dying day. His meanness seemed to me like that of an old cynic; yet his moderation was exemplary, and at last he undoubtedly won the respect of the mother and daughter who waited on him.

CHAPTER I.

EARLIEST TIMES.

WITH reluctance, and with some anxiety, I assume the task of contributing to the fuller knowledge of the late Cardinal. It has been said that if a man has *much in him,* his photograph, taken unexpectedly, will change in moral character so as to seem a different man. Of course, if different passions stir it, this is to be expected. The Oratorians of Birmingham have—some for forty years, a few perhaps longer—seen my brother chiefly as a *leader* or *father*, in bland serenity; in short, in his most amiable aspect. Few Englishmen, indeed, can remember how Oxford and our general public felt towards him fifty years ago, and perhaps think that Oxford *bigotry* did him injustice, and that the kind feeling with which his old College (Trinity) welcomed him somewhat recently, indicated regret at former bigotry. The existing generation has seen him through a mist; and, if my simple statements anywhere clear away that mist, they may almost resent my truth-speaking as an impiety. But if zeal of friends has forced a man into the public gaze, and made him a part of *English history*, future history ought to depict him truly. That I must often disappoint readers is matter of grave sorrow to me.

My two brothers preceded me at the large private school of Dr. George Nicholas, in Ealing, Middlesex, which in my time reckoned 190 pupils. The second brother, Charles Robert, was my senior by three years. The elder, John Henry, already showed marked peculiarities. One point I name first: I cannot remember seeing him at any play, though we had plenty of games. Our ample fives-court was known in all the Middlesex tennis-courts, where the "Nicholas hit" was a current phrase. Our playground was meadow land, slightly rising from a broad strip of fine gravel, where our boys, in large bands, enjoyed Long Rope—with us a glorious game. I now hear of it only as played by small companies of young girls, whose petticoats cripple it. We had cricket and rounders, and in the winter months football; petty fives against every petty wall; hopping and hopscotch, patball and trapball, prisoner's base (or bars?), tops of several kinds, and multiform games of marbles. As far back as my memory reaches, in none of these was John Henry Newman to be seen. He did go to our bathing-pond, but never *swam*. My father took care that he should learn to *ride;* but in literary composition he was very premature, both as to prose and poetry. I happen to remember that before I went to school, and when I hardly can have been full five years old, I acted in our drawing-room the part of *fisherman* to the lord of a (Welsh?) castle. I remember the eulogy put into my mouth on the great lord for "eminence in the four cardinal virtues," and above all, for being *so fond of fish.* It was a little opera written by my premature brother, who must then have been under the age of ten. We three boys, and my eldest sister, Harriett, were all dressed out theatrically, to my father's great amusement. This may have been the *earliest,* but was not at all the *last*, of J. H. N.'s small farces written in his school-days; besides poetry, which, perhaps, was not earlier than his passage from school to college at the too early age of sixteen.

A more characteristic feature of his school-days deserves mention for a special reason. The child, it is said, is father of the man. In imitation of Addison's *Spectator*, J. H. N. commenced a weekly paper, to circulate among his school-fellows; it filled, in manuscript, four moderate pages. I was too young to care about it, but I saw several numbers, perhaps all that appeared. It had an ugly name—*The Spy*. This word may have been his translation of "spectator"; but, many of the boys were made sore by the title, and told me that he *quizzed* everybody. Gradually it leaked out that he had initiated a number of the boys into a special Order, with whom he was every week to read *The Spy*. Among these was my second brother, but I, no doubt, was too young. Charles told me that there were degrees in the Order, marked by ribbons of different colours, with J. H. N. as Grand Master. The society met in one of the vacant rooms of this large school—I think afterwards the French master's. But indignation at the rumour of espionage soon culminated, and the *profanum vulgus* of the uninitiated forced the door open, swept away the faithful officer on guard, seized the papers, and tore off the badges. Thus came the day of doom to *The Spy*. The victors boasted loudly of their triumph, but neither from Charles nor from any of the initiated did I learn intelligible details. Afterwards, I suspected they had taken an oath of secrecy. But some thirty years later, when John had passed into the Church of Rome, my brother Charles wrote, or said, to me that it was just the thing *to be* expected (or, which *he had* expected) from that Ealing affair, for John evidently coveted to be a *Grand Master* of some *Order;* but authority for such a post could only be got from Rome. I by no means give credit to Charles for any long-sightedness, but it was a curious coincidence.

Earlier than 1830, it struck me that prematurity of talent was a great calamity to my very clever brother. He always wanted *balance*. There was nothing boyish, popular, or self-distrusting in his temperament. His taste was fastidious. He could not bear the *coarseness* of the vulgar. In reading History to our family, while my father's business preoccupied him, John often commented severely, especially against the opponents of our Charles I., and against the French Republicans. The "Apologia" fully develops his disgust at the expulsion of a king who had broken his coronation oath, and who was known to be aiming at despotism. My father, whatever his inferiority in culture to his son, had an earnest zeal for *justice*, and in temperament as an arbitrator would have dealt equally with contending parties. But John did not seem to know that a king who claimed *allegiance* must himself be *loyal* and *truthful*, so that duty and right may go hand in hand. But (so it happened) my eldest brother, in my earliest youth, had more influence with me than my father, who was an admirer of Benjamin Franklin and Thomas Jefferson. I had heard him say, "I do not pretend to be a religious man"; also, "I am a man of the world"; nay, once: "I wonder that clever men do not see that it is *impossible* to get back to any certainty where they are so confident"—he meant in *religious history.* So I painfully whispered to myself: "He is not a Christian." But, as I grew up, I began to honour a breadth, serenity, and truthfulness in my father's character. He was rather fond of a coarsely-worded maxim: *Give the devil his due.* After I had outgrown the shuddering at heresy and unbelief (a tedious process with me), I saw him, in my memory, as an unpretending, firm-minded Englishman, who had learned his morality more from Shakspeare than from the Bible, and rejected base doctrine from whatever quarter.*

The main elements of his character were in entire contrast to those of his eldest son. The only quality which I am aware that they had in common was—*love of music.*

When the Coronation of George the IV. was coming into mental view, a widespread excitement dislocated classes and families on

---

* I remember he was shocked at Psalm 109, "Let his prayer be turned into sin," &c.; and Romans 12, "Do good to thy enemy, for it will heap coals of fire upon his head"; and, while he hated sanctimony, he warmly praised, and kept on his special shelf, the volume of Barclay in defence of Quakerism.

the tidings that the King wished to discard his wife, the Princess Caroline, by an odious accusation. In Oxford it caused a battle between Gown and Town. It distracted my father's drawing-room also by a scene which was almost a quarrel, from the vehement part taken by J. H. N. against his father. The Ministry had given notice of prosecution: the trial was begun only. My age was just past fifteen, but the strangeness of the affair was hard to forget, though seventy years have since passed. It would be unfair to my brother to pretend memory of his arguments; yet I may say that I remember none, and can imagine none, except that the fact of the *Ministry* ordering the trial ought to bias us against the Queen. In the altercation between father and son, to reproduce my father's side would be equally futile; only that, on chewing the cud after so painful a duel, I seemed to retain this substance:—

"The Prince, who is now King, overwhelmed with debt, wanted money. The King, his father, forbade Parliamentary aid unless the Prince would marry the Princess

Caroline. But the Prince loved another lady, whom he had married, illegally, yet with all holy rites. To get the money he sacrificed the lady of his love, and accepted the Princess as wife, when he had no *heart* to give her. Of course dislike soon followed; she was unhappy in his home, and virtually was driven into exile. Now, *if it shall be proved* that, scorned by her legal husband, she sought solace from some other lover, hers is a case that deserves great pity, not insult and punishment; and of all living men this King George IV. is the last that has a *right* to censure her."

In my heart I concluded that, after all, my father's argument was *more Christian* than my brother's. But I must add, my father was so irritated that he ended with a sharp sarcasm: "Well, John! I suppose I ought to praise you for knowing how to rise in this world. Go on! Persevere! Always stand up for men in power, and in time you will get promotion." Years afterwards, I discerned that my father had mistaken fanaticism for self-seeking.

Later still, to my surprize, I learned that the Cabinet itself was divided, and that Mr.

Canning had publicly called Queen Caroline *the ornament of her sex.* How wonderful, that J. H. N. at the age of nineteen, and not likely to know *the facts,* all fresh in my father's mind, shall stand up against him thus.

My brother had taken his Bachelor's degree (at least, so I compute) in 1821. Our schoolmaster, Dr. Nicholson, following his own routine, asked him to write the prologue for our midsummer acting of Terence. I was then sixteen, and, as "captain" of the school, had to recite the prologue. Of course, I learned it by heart. I well remember that it was a panegyric on George III., and, as he had been dead eighteen months, the mere fact of my brother selecting this topic, which had nothing to do with Terence, I have thought was notable, since my father and even my father's mother charged George III. as the chief criminal for two cruel, needless wars, both ruinous, the American ignominious also. I *think* my brother's prologue was unbroken panegyric. But this now matters not, since in his "Apologia" his indignation at the expulsion of Charles X. rests on the bare ground that he was a king ; his demerits count for nothing.

So lobsided morality, if propounded in a Mormon Bibli or by a Hottentot Potentate, would be spurned as self-confuted Later I have thought that zeal for authority, as in itself *sacred*, was the main tendency perverting his common-sense.

I went to Oxford in the autumn of 1821, and was lodged with my brother, then a Scholar of Trinity, at Seale's Coffee House. He presently put into my hands a MS. containing his controversy with a fellow-student *against* Baptismal Regeneration. I studied it carefully, but do not remember a word; probably because I was already quite familiar with, and in concert with, every argument. It did not attack *Infant* Baptism. I allude to this because it presently became important.

At Trinity College my brother contracted warm friendship with Mr. John William Bowden, and with him jointly composed a poem on St. Bartholomew's Eve, which was received with glee and admiration in our family.

Since writing the above, I learn that the copyright lasts seven years more, and that I may not reprint the poem, as I had intended, at the end of this volume. It is important that my reader should see what was at this time my brother's sentiment towards Priesthood and his knowledge of Catholic Priests' historical wickedness. Of course each of the two writers held every leading sentiment in common. It suffices to quote a few verses concerning French Catholicism :—

> "Mistaken worship! where the priestly plan
> In servile bondage rules degraded man;
> Where every crime a price appointed brings
> To soothe the Churchman's pride, the sinner's stings;
> Where righteous grief and penitence are made
> A holy market and a pious trade."

The only priest who figures in the poem is a certain Clement, who is depicted as not only a bitter promoter of the perfidious massacres, but as leading a nightly band of assassins.

I rejoice to hear that my brother's Executor will reprint the poem, and that my brother with his own pen has marked his separate share. Mr. Bowden at once fascinated me, as a type of beautiful manhood. It leaked out that his age was now twenty-five. Perhaps he was too tall for an Apollo, but his modest sweetness of expression seemed Christian beauty such as I had not seen in the British Museum from any Greek. I soon read slight verses from his pen, to be sung at the piano, graceful and free. But I scarcely saw him after another year.

In Easter, 1822, my brother was elected Fellow of Oriel, and the kind Dean of the College, the Rev. Endell Tyler,* at once insisted that I should have my meals from Oriel buttery; so we moved into a lodging, still known as Palmer's, in Merton Lane, where we found the Rev. J. Blanco White abiding. He was born twenty-five years before this century, in Spain. His parents were Spanish, but his grandfather Irish. He was a learned priest, and in 1810 had escaped the Inquisition by flight to Lord Wellington's Camp. The Pro-

---

* He was afterwards rector of St. Giles's, London; and, before the late Lord Shaftesbury (then Ashley) was heard of, he opened Baths and Washhouses for the poor. *Endell* Street is called after him. In his long Oxford service he was reputed to be rich for an Oxford Fellow, and his marriage with a Miss Marshall, of Leeds, probably aided his excellent work in St. Giles's. A most instructive sermon from him on "the Lord's Day as *not* the Sabbath," lifted me a first step above the current Evangelicalism.

vost of Oriel (Dr., afterwards Bishop, Copleston) admired him, and invited him to join the Fellows' table; but breakfast and tea he shared with us. He and my brother enjoyed the violin together. I gradually heard their theological talk, which was apt to end by Blanco's sharp warning: "Ah! Newman! if you follow that clue it will draw you into Catholic error." But I believe he meant into self-flagellation, maceration of the body, and unnatural self-hatred, for sinful thoughts, &c. Not having the veteran priest's foresight I was surprized, but not at all alarmed. I had not yet guessed how wide a chasm would soon open between us two. In the "Apologia" his warm love for my brother is quoted in spite of lamented differences.

A word concerning the Rev. Walter Mayers. I must have been under him four years at school after my brother left. He allured me to his new curacy three miles from Deddington, Oxon., to help in Mathematics with his pupils, first in 1822, and again in 1823, after his marriage. (I cannot be accounted *premature;* for, as Aristotle observes, "mature years are wanted to be φρόνιμος, prudent as a statesman, but a boy may be a geometer.") I thus knew Mr. Mayers much better than did my brother, whose few words have been interpreted as though Mr. Mayers were a high Calvinist. Like most other Evangelicals of my youth, his Calvinism consisted in this, that he did not *explain away* the 17th Article, but bowed under it with reverent shuddering. To give prominence to so dreadful a doctrine, and *argue* for it, was against his nature. I am grateful that I learned much from him, and among the rest, to count it duty and wisdom to believe that hereafter we shall be taught some explanation.

CHAPTER II.

1824–33.—FIRST CLERICAL STAGE.

As soon as my brother reached the age of twenty-three he was ordained deacon, which gives the right to preach, if the bishop allow.

Misery was chronic among the silk-weavers of Spitalfields. I was already an eager student of Political Economy; which probably makes me remember that Mr. Huskisson, against a widespread and vehement outcry of frightened tradesmen, had relaxed our tariff against foreign goods, and among others against Italian silk. A great panic arose, probably aided by the alarm in other trades, that the bad state of the silk-weavers would now mount to actual famine; and so it was believed. Whether by Episcopal authority, or in movement initiated by the Clergy, charity-sermons for the starving silk-weavers were announced, and the Rev. Walter Mayers, who highly esteemed my brother's talents, asked him to preach for them,—I think it was his maiden sermon. The young preacher, on accepting, made prominent in his argument, that though to aid a distressed populace was of course right and proper, yet in this case the people threatened with starvation deserved our aid, not only as fellow *men*, but still more as being *Christians*, because they were *baptized*. This was the leading thought, the exact words cannot be recovered; but its doctrine was most perspicuous, that all the Baptized, and only the Baptized, are Christians. In this particular case, Rumour charged the weavers as being largely Atheists. The sudden shock appalled both me and Mr. Mayers. Considering that at my brother's own request I had carefully studied his MS. argument that took precisely the opposite side, I thought it *unnatural* and *ominous* that he had dropt to me no notice and no reason for his momentous change, which to me was like tearing up my first principles. I could not but say to myself, What next? And in this connexion it is easier to say at once, that to his dying day he never gave me any reason, not even when he wished me to take Holy Orders, and cannot have been ignorant that this would be my prominent difficulty, by which, with collateral reasons, I could not help inferring that he *knew* the case from the New Testament to be *rotten*, and that he had no Scriptural argument presentable. His reticence did not at all invite me to consult him.

A second shock came quickly. While I was arranging furniture in my new rooms (1824), I suddenly found a beautiful engraving of the " Blessed Virgin " fixed up. I went to the print-shop and begged its immediate removal, and then learned that my brother had ordered it. I am sure he thought me an ungrateful brother. My own act made me unhappy; yet the more I ruminated, the more I judged that to resist from the beginning was my wisest way. Before he was ordained, our intercourse was comparatively easy, and (I think, but am not sure) on equal terms; so that if he quoted Scripture unconvincingly, I said my say naturally. Since his maiden sermon, I had felt less free. But after *my* repulse of his engraved Virgin, he came out with an attack on *Protestants collectively*, saying that they forgot that sacred utterance, "Blessed art thou among women," and I answered, "Dear John, I do not forget it, but I remember also, that to like words from another woman, Christ replied, '*Yea rather*, blessed are they who hear the Word of God, and keep it.' Our Lord *did not approve* of honouring his mother." He had no reply; but afterwards, I thought, he never argued with me from the Scriptures, but from the Prayer Book; else he talked of Tradition, a word too vague for me to appreciate. I admired the Prayer Book, but knew that in its present form Cranmer and statesmen following him composed it, and *they* did not set it on a par with Holy Writ. Perhaps I now first heard from him, that the New Testament was not *complete without tradition*. But about the Virgin, he returned to the charge, attacking Protestants *in general* as ignorant and hasty; and I gradually thought him to be undermining *every objection* to Invocation of the Virgin.

I suggest to my reader to imagine that my brother, if still alive, might reply " that I misunderstood him: that I ill remember: that I was fanatical against Romanism;" in short, I desire my reader to wait until facts are set before him, and not my memory of things secret between us; yet it would be unnatural not to tell at once how I *saw and felt* in this early stage. His talk had forced me to study Invocation of lower beings, its tendency towards Idolatry, and *why* it was acceptable to low minds, who dared not invoke the Supreme. No worshipper dares to *coax* God Most High, yet a Greek *did* coax "Virgin Artemis," and say, "Dear Goddess! do give me this little favour; it is small for thee to give, but very great for me to get." No Christian dares to entreat *our* God to help him in sin; but if petition be made to any unknown spirit of whose power we cannot guess; to one higher than Man yet not revered as Thrice Holy; this Power is an under-god: and if we think he has answered our prayer, our thanks are to *him*, not to God Most High. Moreover, if we have no *awe* for this under-god, why may we not pray to him as shamelessly as an old Greek to Venus? Years after this, a friend of mine in a clever satire wrote :—

> "The adulterous Knight, to bring his love to pass,
> Invoked the *Virgin's* aid, and vowed a mass."

The more my brother argued about Invocation (not that I dare to say he ever urged me to *practise* it: I think *he stopped short* in refuting my objections) the more uneasy he made me, till one day, wearied with the topic, I broke out in clearer opposition than usual, saying, " But, my dear John, what can be the *use* of invoking a Being who *cannot hear* you? The Virgin is not omnipresent!" He replied, by an argument under which I at once collapsed, muttering inwardly, " What is the use of discussion if he *will* be so *whimsical?*"

The sad importance of this to me was clear when in 1827 I went to Ireland, and saw popular Catholic manuals. From them, I concluded, he had pilfered his arguments.

No doubt I shall be told that these revelations are "unbrotherly." Perhaps they are; but so have been our relations since 1824, sorely against my will. I expected to carry these matters with me into my grave: I never whispered them even to my mother and sisters. To suppress them now there is no motive, when they are only the beginning of a series which made me ashamed of him till he joined the Church of Rome, while I only sighed in secret.

In the "Apologia" he complains that people charge him with borrowing from Romanists arguments which were spontaneous in him. Well; I *tried* to make this allowance in 1827, though to me the coincidence seemed too strong. I certainly do not wish to heap more odium on him than is inevitable. *Grant* that all *was* spontaneous: the sad fact remained, that, *whether he knew it or not*, he was pushing on the Romish line while in the garb of an Anglican. This shocked me greatly. Upon this came, I know not exactly when, his insidious invention of the term Ultra-Protestant to insult all that hold to the cardinal doctrine of Protestantism and common morality. Only when the "Apologia" came out in 1864, had I any idea that with him (p. 197) Protestant and Ultra-Protestant were identical. This invention of two names for the same thing, while the public use only one, *could not* advance Truth, but *might* cunningly aid error. All to me seemed *rotten*. It was at last a relief to me to think him not actually fraudulent, but only fanatical—no vulgar deceiver; and the more acquaintance I made with his conveniently ambiguous words, the more this theory won on me: "He is caught in his own net."

I must add in this stage, that I ill reconcile what I have written, with a statement in his "Apologia." Others will remark on it, if I do not. (Ed. of 1864, p. 87.)

"He (Hurrell Froude) fixed deep in me the idea of devotion to the Blessed Virgin." But J. H. N. knew him only in 1826. Is not this inconsistent with my statement about her in 1824? Apparently; but I have not said that he did more than try to break down my Protestant aversion. And there is another possibility; whether probable the reader may judge. Jesus *himself*, in Luke xi. 28, deprecates calling his mother Blessed, which distinctly forbids devotion as well as invocation: my resistance from the Scriptures *may* have overpowered J. H. N. It was against his nature to say: "On further consideration I find that *you were right, and I was wrong;*" therefore, I *may* have converted him, and never have known it. This would give Hurrell Froude trouble to reconvert him: and what was quite secret between us two, my brother would have no obligation and no reason to tell the public.

In the autumn of 1828 I returned to Oxford, and soon found J. H. N. vicar of St. Mary's and its appanage of Littlemore. His affectionate verses to me on my coming of age (June, 1826) show that he expected me (by the force of sacred habit?) shortly to take Holy Orders; so he gladly used me to call on and look after the poor people at Littlemore. Naturally, I attended his sermons; but never gained from them the instruction or pleasure that others did. *Distrust had sunk roots too deep in me.* To the public, that matters not; but the following has its moral.

Arnold of Rugby, later than this date, commented in a sermon on the deadening effect of a liturgy too often repeated. Oxford students had long felt it; for a current *myth* told of a college chaplain so confident in the tip of his tongue that he challenged all his fellow chaplains to a race, offering to *give them* " up to Pontius Pilate," and boasting that he would clear " St. Chrysostom " before any of them. Of course the satire implied that a chaplain's prayer tended to merge into that of a Tartar's prayer-mill. Various young Evangelicals, known to me, attended my brother's sermons, though not accounting him *sound;* yet in them they found originality and suggestion. Time went forward, and one day they said to me, " What a pity he should have so many churches to serve. Is there no remedy ? " I could not tell what they meant, but soon found that they believed he had three churches to serve in quick succession, and that was why he read with rapidity so painful. When I assured them that the whole story was without basis, my statement amazed them. I now found that my inability to keep up with his pace was shared by others.

I just name this, because he often taunted Evangelical ministers as caring only for their own sermons, and making little of the liturgy. Not that he imputed to *them* any gabbling, but he wanted to reduce the *personal* element required in preaching to its *minimum* (it needed spiritual power), and to raise the *sacerdotal* element, in which the priest was a mere piece of machinery, to its *maximum;* and now I could not help seeing to what his doctrine tended.

In 1829, as a young Fellow, he came out for the first and last time as a canvasser in a popular election. The Duke of Wellington as Premier, and Sir Robert Peel as leader in the Commons, had resolved to propose admission of Romanists into Parliament. Peel had previously been strongly opposed to this measure, while his colleague Canning had insisted that Mr. Pitt's solemn promise, which induced the Irish Parliament to vote its own extinction, had the binding force of a treaty. Now that Peel, after Canning's death, had been converted by events, he honourably resigned his place as M.P., and asked his Oxford constituency to re-elect him. A great ferment arose among them: Sir Robert Inglis was invited to oppose him. An Inglis Committee was formed, of whom my brother was perhaps the youngest and the most active. He told me his reasons for opposing Peel, and I heard them from others; but I *must* not write what I seem perfectly to remember, since it is not in harmony with what I find in the "Apologia" (p. 72, ed. of 1864). Clergymen who came up to Oxford to vote, said to me: We thought we were coming to vote on the question, "What is our duty and wisdom towards Ireland?" but your brother tells us, No! Our only question is, "Does Peel deserve to be re-elected?"

I here quote his own statement (p. 72): "I considered that Mr. Peel had taken the University by surprize; that he had no right to call on us to turn round on a sudden, and to expose us to the imputation of time-serving, and that a great University ought not to be *bullied* even by a Great Duke of Wellington." I venture to ask whether my brother's memory can be perfect? If he had said this, would not the prompt reply have been: " If we expect our M.P. to be frank, we must not allow him to hold contradictory duties. A Cabinet Minister is *bound to secrecy;* if we want openness, it is *our* fault that we elected him." To me this reply seems inevitable. If my brother had argued, "Insist on *no* secrets; *never* elect an office-holder," I might praise his public spirit. But to blame Peel on *this* ground was absurd. Indeed, my memory gives quite another ground. Enough of this quite secondary matter.

Undoubtedly in 1829-30 the perfume of spirituality, with literary beauty and original thought, in the sermons from St. Mary's settled, like dew from heaven, on some older Oxonians, whole or half Evangelical. These from the local committees of the Bible Society and the Church Missionary Society invited my brother, in honorific terms, to join them as a third or second secretary. He at once accepted, and for a short moment they rejoiced. But presently an anonymous pamphlet appeared, of which a copy was sent to every High Church resident clergyman. I heard short questions among our Balliol fellows, with reply by shrug, nod, or wink. At length a copy was handed to me to read. I read it with surprize and suspicion, yet with incredulity. It suggested that every *right-minded* clergyman should just subscribe 10*s.* each to the Bible Society; this would give to each a vote, and enable them collectively to out-vote the present holders of the very ample annual revenue, into which the right-minded would thus simply step. Soon a severe condemnation of this pamphlet came to me from my brother's particular friend, Rev. Samuel (?) Rickards, once a Fellow of Oriel, then a rector in Suffolk. (From him one of my nephews, to whom he was, I suppose, godfather, bears the name John Rickards Mozley.) He called on me in Oxford, lamenting the mess into which he had plunged when the pamphlet was ascribed to John Henry Newman. He thereupon took on himself to deny it right and left, "because," said he, "to speak plainly, it was unworthy of him, and really *mean;* and now comes on me the mortification of having to go round and tell people that after all they were right, and it is your brother's."

I may need to account for Mr. Rickards' familiarity with me, though he was specially my brother's friend, who wrote for Mrs. R.'s album, at Ulcombe, Kent, the piece called Nature and Art in the "Memorials." Mrs. Rickards was a daughter of Sir Robert Wilmot, who had taken a house in Kemp Town near to my mother, then at Brighton. Visiting him, they became well acquainted with my mother and three sisters, and, at the very sudden death of my third sister, Mr. Rickards' deep interest made him almost intimate with them, and on easy terms with me when I returned from Ireland.

J. H. N. had seemed to forget that the Oxford Bible Society was only a *branch*, and that his proposal could only lead to ridicule. In fact he got not a single new 10s. from the "right-minded." Almost simultaneously he made a futile but offensive attack on a much older Evangelical clergyman, who for years had been secretary of the local Church Missionary Society. My brother disliked the habit common to the Evangelical organs, of interlarding their narrative with little phrases from the New Testament. Instead of a few friendly suggestions, he moved in the committee some 255 amendments of his elder colleague's work. To discuss each separately would have been difficult and tedious, if possible, to the committee. To *snub* his elder colleague, who had just taken part in friendly invitation of him, must have destroyed all harmony. He surely ought to have remembered that the elder secretary had borne the work for many years: that his style was a tradition from the Puritans, whose chief classic had been the Bible. The committee was equally divided, and the chairman interpreted the fact as non-approval. On the very next meeting each local society ejected John Henry Newman from his post as secretary, and so the strange episode ended.

In 1829-30 my house-to-house visits in

Littlemore revealed to me the discontent and plentiful vexation at their Vicar's summary claims over the Church music with hymns and psalms. Rustic musicians, who from neighbourly kindness, in a petty church which could not afford an organ, had for years freely contributed their best skill in flute, violoncello, and two other instruments, now received, instead of thanks, a slap in the face by a prohibition to play. (What was his musical substitute, I either did not hear or have forgotten.) That as to the favourite hymns and psalms nobody should in future be consulted or have any function but submission, and that *past custom should go for nothing*, came on them as sudden despotism. It may seem unwise to waste paper and ink on petty matters, but small things may reveal deep tendencies. When I looked at *my brother's conduct from his own point of view*, I thought him suicidal, as I still think. He cannot but have felt that his literary abilities were winning even on the mild elder men of the party which he disliked, and when *they* kindly welcomed him, he was eminently likely to win over the younger, a process which had already begun. Even as to his English style, he did not need to force it forward, as in contumely, on his more venerable joint-secretary, and that by a method most embarrassing to the committee. The elder clergyman would soon have been glad to devolve on the younger all literary work. Patience and time would constantly add to his power. Yet no sooner do events begin to open favourably, than he will not allow his seed to ripen; but, as if a momentary success had intoxicated him, he at once flares into a hostility which looks like treachery. If it were against duty to continue in prudent peace, how easy and how much more politic, as well as Christian, to decline kind offers by saying: "I lament that we differ too much for co-operation." But now he seemed to accept union with set purpose of discord.

To my former judgments of him, these events added something, viz., if the power of Archbishop Laud were yielded to him for a single year, England would soon be in a wild blaze.

My brother for once in his life unbosomed himself to me, and carefully explained the crisis at which he had to resign his tutorship in Oriel College; also the reasons. He was elected Fellow in 1822; now, I think, 1830 was reached. Dr. Hawkins, now Provost, had known him intimately for these years, and was a keen-sighted man. My brother came to him with a novel proposal, enough to startle any head of a college. He said that, as a priest, he was bound to have his main time devoted to religion, and he could not give himself to college teaching unless he might assimilate his pupils to parishioners, and so account them his flock. For this purpose, in his own name and that of two others of the four tutors (viz., Robert Isaac Wilberforce and Hurrell Froude), he proposed that the pupils should be sorted into four equal bodies so that each tutor should be in the position of curate to one quarter of the pupils, and separately responsible for their spiritual guidance. Dr. Hawkins refused on the ground that its tendency was to set up in a college, instead of *one* Anglican Church, *four* separate sects with perhaps a sensible diversity of Creed. His consent could not be gained. Thereupon the *three* concordant tutors resigned simultaneously, and the Provost was driven to severe straits. To take a tutor from another college was in those days unheard of. It was to me a singularly new form of *strike*,* and the strikers seemed to hold the winning hand. But I can hardly doubt Dr. Hawkins saw that each tutor would become a *father confessor* and that he *must* at any risk, and with any loss, refuse to be coerced. Rev. Joseph Dornford, the eldest tutor, stuck to him, the nephew of Bishop Copleston accepted his invitation, and Hawkins probably resumed his old function of tutor; thus somehow, like a ship with broken sails and a jurymast, his college for several months weathered the gale.

Let me for a moment widen my view to the Pusey-Newman movement.

INCIDENTAL AIDS TO PUSEYITE SUCCESS.

Lord Grey, in 1832, carried his Reform Bill, which could not help strengthening the Dissenters in Parliament. Alarm concerning Catholics, from their admittance in 1829, *was still alive* in the Anglican Clergy, whose fears

* Perhaps the word in this sense arose in 1837.

ejected Peel from his Oxford constituency. The claim of Protestant Dissenters for separation of Church and State was presently vexatious to Lord Grey, the Premier. Eight Irish bishoprics (if my memory is correct) were abolished by Parliament, which to Rev. Mr. Keble and my brother seemed a *sacrilege*, " a national apostacy." Lord Derby, father of the present Earl, and Sir James Graham, presently left the Whig party in alarm for the tithes. The abolition of bishoprics showed that the Anglican Church was the *creature* of the State; which might repeal or modify the Act which had ejected the Presbyterian Clergy. To open the Established Church was a terrible thought, but Dissenters had not asked it. They had claimed *Separation* : that was the pressing danger. Puseyites exalted the Church, against the State, claiming its aids and honours as a thing of course, without conditions. Towards Dissenters they thought contempt better than argument.

Oriel College is rector of the Oxford parish of St. Mary, and, as rector, appointed my brother vicar to the parish church; that is, caretaker of the souls of the *non-academical*

D—2

parishioners. The University at a distant time had repaired or rebuilt St. Mary's Church, and thus acquired the right of occupying it for University sermons at a different hour from the parish services. My brother, as vicar of the parish, preached to the local tradesmen and the College servants; but our English public supposed him to be the weekly preacher to the *Academics by University appointment*. This natural mistake immensely enhanced his importance, even to numbers of the country clergy. An old British clergyman said to me in the winter of 1834-5: "Well! though one cannot accept many things from those 'Tracts for the Times,' I am glad to see somebody at last standing up for our old Church. It is too bad to see her subjected to *we know not what* from Dissenters in Parliament." Such undoubtedly was a widely prevalent feeling.

I continue *this topic* by a great jump of chronology. After Bishop Colenso found himself liberated from clerical bonds and allegiance to the Bishop of Cape Town by the decision of the Privy Council that Parliament had *forgotten* to enslave the African clergy, Dr. Pusey, in public meeting with his clerical friends, *thanked God* that the African Church was *free from the yoke of the State.* Having gone myself to Birmingham to see my brother, I caught at this piece of news as a topic of talk with him; for to find anything to say that might not grate on him was a hard task. He replied almost gaily, "Oh! it is only what I expected." I was surprized, but he continued, "When in 1833 we met to start the 'Tracts for the Times,' we thought it only prudent to be frank to one another, and we all submitted to free questioning on every important subject: among them, the Union of Church and State. To our astonishment we found that, one and all, we desired entire separation. The book on Scotch Episcopalianism (ascribed to Archbishop Whately) had converted us." "Is this a secret?" asked I. "Not at all," was his reply, "tell it as widely as you choose." I am amused to find, that while the clergy were looking to the Puseyites as their defence against the formidable Dissenters, those very Puseyites were on the side of the foe. I since find in the "Apologia" the aversion of my brother in 1833 to a State Church.

Nor are Evangelicals eager to retain it. One college friend of mine a little before his death said: "I suppose separation of Church and State *must* come. I dare not wish for it; I cannot foresee the results; but the only good of the Establishment that I have known is: *It has saved me from the enmity of my bishop.*" Another college friend of mine who became Bishop of Bombay said to me in earlier days: "You see, the best intentioned English statesmen had too difficult a task in the Reformation, so many were to be pleased. They had a *bad job* before them; necessarily our Anglican Church is the best of a bad job." To my prosaic mind, these quiet people, who, without hypocrisy, try to make the best of imperfect human work, are much wiser than poetical minds which rave as if what can only be human *ought to be* divine.

ANOTHER COINCIDENCE.

Another incident was favourable to the Puseyites, on which Professor Baden Powell commented to me, perhaps thirty-five years ago. His avowed strength was in practical

Optics and observation of the shooting stars, concerning which he largely added to our modern theory; but he also was a keen student of Primary Axioms, and an effective writer against the foundation of Puseyism. He gave me quite a new idea of Lloyd, Bishop of Oxford, and told me that but for his lamented sudden death two men so young as my brother and Pusey never could have exercised such power in Oxford as they did. I just knew that Lloyd was a learned man, and very genial in deportment. He kindly twitted a young Evangelical clergymen, by asking him " whether he called the Sunday *Sabbath;*" a piece of ignorance much despised by the Oriel Fellows, and named by Continental Protestants, " Figmentum Anglicanum." Lloyd was the Regius Professor of Divinity as well as Bishop. I now learned from Baden Powell that he was learned in German theological literature, and felt it a scandal that in Oxford there was a total absence of solid learning as to the origin and history of the separate books of our Scriptures. He was bent to remedy this by promoting classes of Scriptural study after taking the Bachelor's degree.

As Theological Professor he could not enforce anything hastily; but he took all the first steps and expected to win support gradually. But before they could be at all opened, he died most unexpectedly. His successor in the bishopric, like most of the elder men, had no enthusiasm that could attract young men— no dash, no show of self-sacrifice. The result was that whatever Lloyd had begun aided the movement of Newman and Pusey towards a goal almost opposite; which, if Lloyd had lived, it is doubtful whether against his age, sound learning, high character, and double office, they would have had any noticeable success. (I write not from any knowledge of Bishop Lloyd; but since Baden Powell's opinion interested me, it may interest my readers also. I do not know the year of Lloyd's death, perhaps 1831 or early in 1832.)

Few can now know the first public steps of Dr. Pusey. Perhaps in 1825, when a Fellow of Oriel College, he went to Germany for the study of Hebrew and Arabic, and on his return to Oxford was appointed by the Duke of Wellington to the post of Regius Professor of

Hebrew, by the advice (it was supposed) of Lloyd, Bishop of Oxford. He wrote two good-sized pamphlets on modern German Theology, which delighted me. He warmly defended (in 1828-30) the piety of the Germans; but Mr. Hugh Rose, of Cambridge, thought that Bishop Lloyd needed to teach him the superiority of an Episcopalian to a Presbyterian. I had several pleasing talks with him, and remember how earnestly he pressed that our missionaries should well understand the *minds* of natives; so as to know what points *they held in common*. I found nothing fanatical in him then. But when I came back to England in 1833, he was in appearance a wholly changed man; but I had no means of judging why. Because he was a Regius Professor the public invented the name *Puseyite*. Nevertheless I have thought that his knowledge of German made him incapable of close sympathy with my brother's procedure. The statements in the "Apologia" now suggest to me that he took no part in the " Tracts for the Times."

FANATICISM.

I cannot despise sincere fanaticism: *it often*

is a great power. In the new Salvationists I alternately censure it and admire it. Knots which mild wisdom cannot untie, fanaticism, like some fierce war, will sometimes cut. Warm enthusiasm is excellent in youth, yet easily degenerates into fanaticism; easily too, it is wrongly imputed by those who are too selfish to feel enthusiasm. Moreover, when fanaticism enters a whole band, though its power is immensely increased, yet culpability of individuals is much lessened. When it forgets Justice, one must not palliate it. Also, Puseyism did not *begin* with my brother, but with old Alexander Knox, a pious admirer of Wesley, who condescended to give me several private talks in Ireland. I cannot join any of the *panegyrics* on my brother; yet he was certainly a *high-minded* fanatic in regard to money. My second brother, Charles Robert, has been brought in of late, and I name him here, to repeat his words: " John ought to have been a Prince; for he always spends money like a Prince." Out of his poverty John spent first on me; I need not speak of others. Baroness Coutts of late extolled the late Cardinal for " Purity, which belongs to no one Creed." I can only interpret *Purity* here to mean *faithful use of trust-money*, of which this wealthy and generous lady has much experience, no doubt. How matters *now* move in dignified Church circles I cannot know; but sixty and more years ago, on the death of a bishop or dean the chief interest seemed to turn on the income smiling on the successor: I mean, in the *High* Church. Whether from my brother came their name, "High and Dry," I am not aware, but he certainly treated the zeal for Church Pelf with *a lofty scorn;* so did his friend Pusey, who, out of his moderate private fortune, gave £1,000 on a single occasion. Thenceforward (my brother told me) "the purses of the laity were opened, and we never wanted money." The temperament (as far as I know) of all so-called Puseyites was (to cut words short) financially noble. The late Cardinal, in my belief, was honoured among his near friends for this temperament. Naturally, it aided his influence beyond that narrow circle.

J. H. NEWMAN'S STRONG AND WEAK POINTS.

No panegyric of late has been to me so

weighty as that of my friend J. A. Froude, concerning my brother's admirable power as a lecturer on Scripture History. I never heard him in a class. I have often heard the remark, that if he had become a barrister, whether in Common Law or Chancery, he would have been eminent among the few. This exactly strikes off my belief. His fine taste and " subtlety " would have suited Chancery, and from Cicero he had learned the art of pommelling broadly enough for any Jury. He urgently needed a thesis to attack or defend, some authority as the goal of his eloquence, or *concessions* made by another : then he had a start. In his conversation, as soon as he had extracted adequate concessions, he was a powerful reasoner, entangling, like Socrates, the unwary disputant. Not from any talent in me, but barely from the fact that he could get no concessions out of me, I always found his arguments puerile. My sole concession was the *paramount supremacy* of Christ and the New Testament ; which never helped him, but rather was felt by him awkward: for I had studied the New Testament and the Psalms from an earlier age than he. When he had to prance with a young Anglican priest, he was soon on galloping ground. He then could quote: "Receive thou the Holy Ghost. Whose *sins* thou dost *forgive*, they are forgiven; whose *sins* thou *retainest*, they are retained. Is this solemn and Divine truth? If not, *it is gross indefensible hypocrisy and falsehood.* To take that alternative is impossible. *Your honourable and high position forbids it,*" &c., &c. Once give him this start, and he unrolled the whole skeleton of virtual Popery, as our Anglican doctrine, before his respondent had any idea into what the discussion would carry him. If he had *tried* to tamper thus with me (who had *not* received the divine prerogative), he might expect the reply: " But, my dear John! *when* did that form of Ordination first come into the Church? Christ says: 'I am He that openeth, and no man can shut; or shutteth, and no man can open.' This shows that he never meant to give such power to mortal man, much less to a possibly wicked priest." Ever since his first sermon he never could get *any starting-point* from me. His weakness and credulity as to *First Principles* were to me lamentable. Indeed, his early zeal for ghost stories may have been at the bottom.

I remember that at Brighton one year he kept us all agog by a tale of ghosts which seemed inexplicable except by believing in the spirits; then, after two or three weeks, he suddenly told us he had found it all to be false. I suppose he was ashamed; for he would not tell us either how he had been deluded or how undeceived. But that an educated man, not reared in Egypt or Abyssinia, should believe that an outward touch, whether by consecrated oil or a holy thumb, could affect the state of the soul and its acceptance with its Supreme Lord, seemed to me as base a folly as any magic. He did not see, that to deny such occult power is *now* a reasonable First Principle.

I may say (without danger of imputing what he possibly could contradict or modify), that he once playfully challenged me to what I may call, A Game of Sham Logic. " Of course, First Principles *cannot be proved* (wrote he); therefore, in order to try what will come of it, we may assume anything. Let me then assume that the Pope is *our divinely-appointed leader* to Truth." [I cannot be sure that I rightly quote to the letter the words in italics: that matters not.] I replied substantially as follows : " Most truly you say, that no First Principle can be *proved*, if proof means deduction : but it ought to be *approved*, else its assumption is not only futile, but throws dust into our eyes. Your assumption is to me arbitrary and unplausible ; as, probably, you would say, if I proposed to you playfully to assume as a First Principle that the Grand Llama of Thibet is our divinely-appointed teacher."

He gave no reply, and I could not guess at what he was driving. He asserted nothing ; therefore, if still alive, he never could say I had not represented his assertion fairly. I only wondered whether such proposals were a specimen of his philosophy.

FIRST PRINCIPLES.

I am seduced into a digression " on my own hook," as our Americans speak. First Principles are *shifty* matters, both with nations and with persons. Each individual picks them up from his birth and birthplace ; and they enter all common beliefs. In a stagnant nation, they change little in many generations, but when in literature knowledge accumulates, the principles current shift gradually, just as England was not the same under Edward I. and Edward VI. Similarly, each person now in England starts with First Principles imparted traditionally from his "surroundings," but as knowledge becomes wider, and thought more active, new first principles, like new leaves on a tree, push off the old ones as superfluous; because truths can now be received as axioms, which in younger days were by no means so clear. This (I think) is peculiarly true of *Negative* propositions. *Credulity* in the untaught savage, as in the child, mars his good sense, nay, depraves his morals; as when a belief in witchcraft leads native American tribes to burn to death on suspicion a hapless man or woman. To unlearn traditional folly may be the *first necessary* wisdom.

"Sapientia prima est stultitia caruisse."

An incredulity *which admits exception* may be in an earlier stage a young man's starting-point. Increased experience may at length be intensified into *absolute* incredulity, which virtually is equivalent to a new axiom, as in the rejection of all miracles *reported by mere hearsay*, of which we cannot cross-examine the first witnesses. Abundant instances exhibit as a fact that thus new and new inquiry raises up new starting-points. This difference of mind from mind as to First Principles constantly makes religious controversy futile.

CHAPTER III.

HIS MISSION TO *de*-PROTESTANTIZE US.
1832-1842.

AFTER my return from Turkey in 1833, I found my brother's book on the Arians in my mother's house. Only one passage struck me, and that only do I remember. In writing against Arius, the elder bishop against whom Athanasius at length prevailed, my brother depreciated the authority of Fathers *earlier* than Athanasius, because *the Church had not yet taught them how to express themselves:* I feel myself audacious in here trusting my memory, for I have never seen the book since that one glance at it. But I have no time to lose now. He was an early bookworm in Gibbon : Gibbon's sly quotation from a Popish historian had taught him that Romanist erudition pronounced *all* the *Ante-Nicene* Fathers unsound. *Therefore* now my brother unceremoniously sweeps them away. Whither is his logic gone? thought I. He is like the man who mistakes on which side he ought to saw off a branch, and saws off the side on which he is sitting! My brother has worried me with *Tradition*, and now, by cutting away the first three centuries, he leaves no *Tradition* at all, but only the sectarian broils of fierce fanatics who fought with more or less aid from the unbaptized Constantine. His argument cuts its own throat. His justification (not from Gibbon, but from his own sagacity) amused me. The *Church* had not *taught* the Fathers of the three first centuries how to express themselves! Might he not similarly depreciate St. Paul? What Church existed in the first ages except these very Fathers whom it is dangerous forsooth to quote as authorities? I since make sure that in his book on Development he has earned praise for "subtlety" by defending what to my blunt mind is monstrous: but to deny that he cuts himself off from Tradition is impossible.

On first confronting my brother on our joint return from abroad, his dignity seemed as remarkable as his stiffness. Somebody (perhaps one of my Evangelical friends) told me he had said: Excommunication of me was superfluous, for I had excommunicated myself. Cleverly invented, if false. I had committed the sin of communicating *with Baptists*, and he must have well guessed that we were far worse than silly in accepting as meant for *us* the words of Jesus: "Where two or three meet in my name, there am I in the midst of you"; solemn words, which with us superseded Priesthood.*

I had already got into disgrace, which soon became worse and worse, because I did not accept the Sibboleth, Jesus *is* Jehovah; and as my brother must have studied the question for his "Arians," I thought it might seem kind to plead for aid from his learning. I am bound to say, that to every practical question he replied kindly, if stiffly; he taught me what were the less guilty *Semi*-Arians, assured me that the Nicene Creed was *abundantly*

---

* Not that we despised priestly teaching. But as Mr. Senior graduated *shoes*: To the Englishman, a necessary; to the Scotchman, a decency; to the Irishman, a luxury; so, I suppose, we held Priests to be never necessary; for the Sacraments always a decency; in a pulpit, sometimes a high luxury.

enough for my orthodoxy, and that the Evangelical formula pressed on me was rank Heresy!

There was a slap for Evangelicals! *Jehovah-Jesus*, I think, is a popular hymn. A kind and learned *lay* Congregationalist assured me that the Nicene Creed was a great mistake. Somewhat later I heard that the Rev. Moses Stuart (of Andover in America) regarded it as certain that unless European Metaphysics or Philosophy could go back to " Emanations " we cannot recover the position of the Nicenists.

An Evangelical critic, immediately after the recent funeral, quoted the Cardinal's emphatic, and publicly uttered, *contempt* of Evangelicals. It may not be amiss to state its grounds as far as I know them.

(1.) Because this school seems habitually to assume, that no one who does not hold their creed knows anything of inward religion, nor is a true Christian. For this insolence he fixed on them the epithets, *prigs* and *priggists*.

(2.) For their obstinate ignorance of the history of the Christian Lord's Day, or Sunday, as an institution having no point in common with the Hebrew Sabbath. They aggravate their *ignorance* into *fraud*, by perversely misusing the word Sabbath to mean Sunday, and this goes not only against history from the Apostles' day till John Knox, but against the New Testament, against Luther and Calvin, and against the name given to the English Saturday in Arabic, in Italian (Sabat, Sabato) even in *French* Samedi, for Sabadi. They persevere in the *fiction* that the Apostles changed the Fourth Commandment, in spite of protest from the Continental Protestants, and, after importing the fraudulent sense of Sabbath from Scotland, have propagated it in England, and carried it into Switzerland.

(3.) On the matter of the Trinity, they fancy themselves wise, while they are really flat Heretics condemned by the old Councils.

On the third count, I plead for them from the Council of Trent. These Protestants *mean* to obey the Church! Their "heresy" is a fruit of honest dulness which is at bottom *implicit* (*i.e.*, virtual) *faith*. I am not condemning; not I. But a far better defence with me is, when I see them so eagerly preoccupied with labouring and self-denying good works, that they *have not time* to examine the historical grounds of their faith. They are the largest part of the Salt which saves England from corruption, despise them who may.

The next revelation came to me from two hymns written by my brother on his return home from Italy in November and December, 1832. They are two out of more. They were printed, but *perhaps* not published till later. I think I met them in my mother's house. I was shocked at them. How could he believe himself a faithful Anglican? And why did he not himself give me a copy? He perhaps knew my temperament and distrusted it. As a little boy, I was a rattling talker; and if a gentleman petted me, I was soon on his knee, quite at home; and my father said of me to my mother before the family: "Never tell a secret to that boy, for it will be sure to leak out from him." That, by the way. However, when I afterwards put these hymns side by side with the wild violence of my brother against Mr. Kingsley, it seemed to me almost an insanity.

PRIVATE JUDGMENT.

1. Poor wanderers! ye are sore distrest
   To find that path which Christ has blest,
     Track'd by his saintly throng.
   Each claims to trust his own weak *will*:
   Blind idol! so ye languish still,
     All wranglers and all wrong.

2. He saw of old and met your need,
   Granting you Prophets of His creed
     The throes of fear to swage (*sic*).
   They fenc'd the rich bequest He made,
   And sacred hands have safe convey'd
     Their charge from age to age.

3. Wanderers! come home, obey the call—
   A *Mother* pleads, who ne'er let fall
     One grain of holy Truth.
   Warn you and win, she shall and must;
   For now she lifts her from the dust
     To *reign* as in her *youth*.

December, 1832.

On this, one may ask: (1) Is it consistent with Anglican doctrine? (2) or with the New Testament? (3) or with good sense?

We have a right to ask (2) because it says, Christ gave us *Prophets*, which can only mean Apostles, who wrote Sacred books, and the Bequest can only mean the New Testament.

But the New Testament tells us *nothing* of a Holy Mother who is to reign over us, but who reappears in the following hymn.

(3.) This hymn identifies following Private Judgment with following that Blind Idol, one's own *weak will*. The writer seems to me never to have known what it is to search after truth. How else could he be ignorant that the searcher after truth seeks for *evidence*, and constantly sacrifices Prepossessions and his own Will in the search. So to brand Private Judgment is a confession that he has never known what it is to search for truth deliberately.

(1.) The hymn is addressed to Protestants, and the career of the writer attests that he especially aims at Anglicans. Nonconformists who disown the Anglican formula of Priest-making were always to him game too well armoured for any fundamental attack.

Anglican *clergymen* are not at all excluded in this hymn. A Holy Mother, *as in her youth*, is shortly to *reign* over all. That era is here pointed at. Hildebrand is suggested by History, and apparently seven high Dignitaries of the Anglican Church are *all wranglers and all wrong!* Religious thought which deals with an unseen spiritual world cannot always be harmonious in human minds; but to call us "all wranglers" is *untrue*, " and all wrong " is *immodest*, contemptuous and eminently self-conceited. But let us pass to another hymn, strangely called

PERSECUTION.

1. Say, who is he, in deserts seen
   Or at the midnight hour,
Of garb austere, and dauntless mien,
Measur'd in speech, of purpose keen,
Calm as in heaven he had been,
   Yet blithe when perils lour?

2. My Holy Mother made reply:
   " Dear child! it is my Priest.
" The world has cast him forth, and I
" Dwell with wild earth and gusty sky.
" He bears to men *my mandates high*
   " And works *my sage behest*.

3. " Another day, dear child! and thou
   " Shalt join *his* sacred band.
" Ah! well I deem, thou shrinkest now
" From *urgent* rule and *severing vow*—
   " Time hath a taming hand."

November, 1832.

To Christianity this creed has no likeness. It sets up a new Deity, called "Holy Mother," who gives mandates to a Priest. He is to tame us into dear obedient children, and (apparently) into monks, nuns, and celibate clergy. But its elements are essentially Romanist, *anything* but Protestant or sound morality. The Mother would be *in nubibus* without the solid Priest walking on earth, such as Rome affords,—a Director in flesh and blood. But Jesus of Nazareth *distinctly forbids* such a functionary.

"Call no man Guide (or Director) on earth, for one is your Director, *even Christ*; and all ye are brethren."

Christ forbids the very thing (an authoritative Director) to which J. H. Newman, of his own "Blind *will*" and fantasy, commends us to listen. We are to resign our consciences to a church officer!

There is so much to say against a doctrine which subverts morality, common sense, and the words of Jesus as told in the New Testament, that we are in danger of overlaying the main offence by too many secondary arguments. Therefore I am cautious. But I may ask:

Did J. H. N. while in the Anglican Church *publish* that he hated Protestantism, both name and thing? Until the "Apologia" came out I thought he retained the name, in opposition to his *ultra* Protestantism.

Further: Did he defend himself by saying: "Not one of the Thirty-nine Articles *commands* us to use Private Judgment, or *forbids* me to denounce it"? As well might he expect every axiom of morals to be set down there, as the axiom, "*No man can cast off on to another his duty* to choose between right and wrong, and his *responsibility* for his choice."

Both in these hymns, and in the "Apologia," J. H. N., p. 117, avows his utter renunciation of Protestantism and of Private Judgment in 1833. Yet ("Apologia," p. 6, ed. of 1864, and elsewhere) he resents as a slander Kingsley's imputation, "that I *was secretly a Catholic*, when I was openly professing to be a minister of the Established Church."

If his denial turns on the word *secretly*, might we not have expected him to emphasize it, thus:

"*Not* 'secretly.' *All who care to inquire* might know, that I abjured Protestantism and Private Judgment; and as to my being a Catholic, that is an unfair word to use, for readers will interpret it as Papist, but my doctrine was *then* only Romanist, not Papist."

But if that was *not* his meaning, I must leave my readers to solve the enigma, as they best can. It surpasses my power.

My secret comment on these two hymns dates from 1833, when I first had copies of them. They were only two out of the *Lyra Apostolica:* I never cared to read more. My grief and indignation is in 1890 long ago faded and stale, yet resumes its place in my heart, when I am forced to dwell on such utterances from an Anglican priest. I long hoped to be for ever as silent to the public concerning them as I was carefully reticent to my brother. I could not guess what made his sense of *Truthfulness* so different from mine; and, if forced to clash with him face to face, Reconciliation, I felt, would never in our life be possible. I resolved to deal with him, if I had sufficient self-control, as if he had been my father. I think I did so to his life's end. As matters now stand, I must not speak doubtfully where I have no doubts; but I try rather to call my readers to judge from the facts as I recite them.

I see that in "Apologia" (p. 118) my brother attacks me in these short words: "St. Paul bids us avoid those *who cause divisions:* you cause divisions: therefore I must avoid you." I think that he here transfers into fact his own inward thoughts. If he had said such words to me I should certainly have replied: "My dear John, tell me *how, where,* and *when* I have caused divisions? It is the very opposite of my earnest desire. I should blame myself vehemently if I were guilty of it." And *he would have had no reply* (in 1833 to 1845 at least), as I will now show my readers. In Dublin (1827-8) I for the first time entered a Nonconformist Church, led in by others. It was called Mr. Kelly's. I did not *cause division*—it was *already* made. The same remark holds of other (orthodox) Churches, especially Baptists, to whom I joined myself in 1835 or '36, and the only part which I took was, to support Union with Pædo-Baptists, *not* to divide. In 1833, the year to which he seems to refer, my zeal was for Union of *all* (Protestant) Christians, remaining in their own connexions; as to which I at once met a mournful disappointment. If my brother had shown me as much courtesy as did my *tutors* at Worcester College, or my senior Fellows at Balliol, instead of tormenting me by chidings as if I were a young child, he might have known me better.

He accepted ordination in the Anglican Church of his own free-will, knowing its history, and that it was established, not by Cranmer and his clergy, but by Henry and his Lay Parliament, before whom the clergy were as powerless as Bp. Fisher had been. If he accepted Priesthood in such a Church, and vowed sincere belief in the book of Common Prayer, the universal understanding of common morality (*and of my morality*) was that he acquiesced in its practically-established rule, both as to the *Government* of the Church and as to its doctrines—so far as it spoke with a single voice.

While each clergyman strives to retain the truths clear to his own mind, he deserves respect and pity as to the self-contradictions of our Prayer Book. My brother grieved me by suddenly turning round with graceful ease; and, dogmatically propounding as sacred truths the very reverse of what he had held before his Ordination, he treated the authorities of his own Church, the Bishop of London, I now find, as well as the Grey Ministry, with more than contempt, for the suspicion that they desired to lessen the difficulties of the Evangelicals, and *might* desire to make the Church more *National*. This seems to me the reverse of right.

So secret was he to me, that I did not know *our agreement* that the Church ought not to be united to the State. We developed the idea in opposite directions. He desired ("Apologia," p. 113) to return not to the *sixteenth* century, but to the *seventeenth*, which can only mean, to the times of Archbishop Laud. My desire was, to let all read the New Testament *with fresh eyes*, not preoccupied by human dogma. I wanted the doctrine of Christ himself. If we could not get it from the *first* century, I saw no chance of getting it from the fourth nor from the seventeenth. But my brother never imparted to me any of his reasons; therefore those will be disappointed who now expect that I can reveal them. The moment he knew that the break-up of the vile system of POCKET BOROUGHS would admit our great Manufacturing Cities into Parliament, he conceived such a hatred of Liberal Ministers that he thought resistance to their legitimate rule to be heroism, and ascribed to them projects which (he informs us) made him " fierce." Submission to Authority is no longer a duty in his eyes, but he adopts Keble's phrase, " National Apostasy," as fitly describing the abolition of Bishoprics judged superfluous by those above him in *Church* government. But he knew, when he took Orders, that this was the Established system.

So far his conduct appeared to me to be almost factious and seditious, which was just *what Paul meant* by " Heretical." But in the two hymns a far more grave offence opens itself. He destroys the *foundation* of the Anglican Church, the right of the Laity to separate from a false Priesthood, commonly called the *right and duty* of Private Judgment. This denies the Anglican Church to have any Christian basis, and (inasmuch as Morals were earlier than Christianity) absurdly forbids conversion to Christ from any foreign religious system. His hymn vitiates his "Orders" by denying the Protestant foundation. Moreover, he attacks the Anglican Episcopate as "all wranglers and all wrong."

To me it was a plain fact that these two hymns taught full-blown Romanism. *Urgent Rule* and *Severing Vow* gratuitously go forward into monkery, nunnery, and celibate clergy. I do not forget that in a later year he set forth that he had not been teaching Popery, but only Catholicism; yet, whether you look out on a real or on a theoretical Europe, the distinction is impossible. If the laity are to submit, not to their own consciences as influenced by the Spirit of God (or Christ), but to a Priest under guidance from a Holy Mother (in the clouds?), then to *which* Priest? Are all Priests concordant? If there is to be Unity, in his sense, must not all Priests be subject to a Central Priesthood, which is nothing but a Papacy? He establishes slavery for the disciples instead of, as the decisive matter, the equality announced to all by Jesus; a *corporate* relation to God, instead of one PERSONAL and spiritual, as taught by Jesus.

Evidently, if Pagans have any moral right

to leave their native Paganism, allured by nobler and purer truth in a communion called Christian, they retain the very same right and duty to leave the latter, when it lapses into new Paganism. To deny Private Judgment to laymen is to forbid passing from an inferior religion to a nobler.

Wonderful it was to me that my brother could (as it were) *forge* the name of Jesus to the prohibition to judge for oneself and to the imposition of a " Holy Mother." He knew he hated Protestantism, but instead of quitting at once the *Protestant* Church, he fancied he might stick to it as long as he preferred an impossible Archbishop Laud to an actual Roman Pope; instead of leaving it (as so many of the Evangelicals) while he could do so, without compulsion.

ANGLICAN INCONSISTENCIES.

A clergyman, more eminent than most of our bishops, freely propounded to me, perhaps in 1841, the clerical dilemma, and his solution of it, thus : The history of our Church counts from the Reformation. Neither Cranmer nor the Ministers of Edward VI. could bear to eject from Church office the elder clergy ; also they knew that the laity, however they might hate clerical extortion or vice, were not yet ripe for very decisive change in creed. Hence with kind intention they left many a germ of Romanism in the Liturgy or the Rubrics, and unawares made our formularies sometimes obscure, sometimes inconsistent. No doubt they expected that in the next generation a more complete revision and reform would be made; *and so it ought to have been*, but with Queen Mary's allegiance to Rome, Elizabeth's ambition, and next the Stuarts, the formularies have been nailed down on us half-reformed, and variously self-refuting. Now it is *impossible* for any man to believe at once two things contradictory; therefore our only possibility is, to inquire which of them we *can* believe, and take no notice of the rest.

This gentleman had no element of a fanatic in him. I respected him too much to utter what rose in my heart. "What a cruel trap to a man's conscience does your Church set!"

An inquiry arises: Did all the Puseyites see those two hymns? I pass over the rest. Were all who saw them so blind as not to see the intense and flippant scorn which they uttered against all Protestantism, including Anglican bishops? Did they share that scorn, and believe that it was exactly the right sentiment for an Anglican priest?

I can only reply *tentatively*, by guesses: (1) Very few copies of these hymns may have been printed privately. Only few Puseyites may have seen them. In an advertisement, I have lately seen that they are *re*-printed. (2) I have professed above that the more widespread a fanaticism, the less is the responsibility of each individual. (3) I digress to exhibit proof of the fanaticism then reigning. Hurrell Froude died prematurely. Keble and my brother became joint editors of his MSS., and apologized for giving prominence to so *young* a man, who had never held *any ecclesiastical* office, but, they add, the *singular truth* of his writings justifies it. [Let any one who can, correct me if I have not remembered the phrase *singular truth;* for I have not seen the book since that first day.] After this in preface, the two editors laid before us his utterance of hatred against the French for dethroning Charles X., which I remember as:

"I hope that the march of mind in France will yet prove A BLOODY ONE."

More than once I had heard such extravagances from Hurrell Froude, and thought him to be sportively "playing the young man," νεανιευόμενος, and never imagined that he could be serious. But what of the two editors, that they were not shocked?

In the "Apologia" Hurrell Froude is held up in surprising eminence. Let us hear some of his virtues (p. 85) :—" He professed openly *his admiration of the Church of Rome*, and *his hatred of the Reformation.* He delighted in . . . sacerdotal power and full ecclesiastical *liberty* (*i.e.*, liberty to persecute). He had a high severe idea of the *intrinsic excellence* of virginity. He embraced the principle of penance and mortification. He had a devotion to the *real Presence.* He was powerfully drawn to the Mediæval Church, *but not to the Primitive*" (p. 86).

Reader! how tired you are of all this! So am I. Why should we not laugh together when a thing is really laughable? There is relief in a hearty laugh. You remember the showman with his box and spy-glass, through which children look to see inside Blücher and Wellington with other officers after the battle of Waterloo. Of him a little boy asked: "Which is the Duke and which is Blücher?" The showman replies: "Whichever you please, my little dear; you pays your penny and takes your choice."

This fairly typifies the relation of "the Holy Mother" to Hurrell and John Henry Newman. They ask her, "Which is the Starting Era of Orthodoxy? We two are puzzling about it." John Henry Newman says, the Nicene Church; Hurrell thinks it is at Hildebrand's, seven hundred years later. The Holy Mother replies, "*Wherever you please*, my little dears; you pay allegiance to me, and take your choice—anywhere *except* too near to Christ and the Apostles, for *they* cut *me* out entirely."

Their unanimous aversion to the Primitive Church, which has no element of Sacerdotalism, denoted that neither of them had any *desire* to ascertain what Jesus and his Apostles taught, on whose names they were riding.

When a mortal believes himself called to a Divine Mission, it is hard to avoid elation, and perhaps arrogance. But if the direction of his course is beneficial and humane, we dare not censure. I have had more than a few indications which denote that my brother's claims went beyond sobriety. Domestic matters I will not tell, except to add my sister's emphatic testimony: "John *can* be most amiable, most generous. He can win warm love from all his friends: but to become his friend, the essential condition is, that you see everything along his lines, and accept him as your leader."

Here I ask leave to digress in defence of my mother and sisters, whom my *brother-in-law*, my sister Harriet's husband, strangely misrepresented in his Memorials of Oxford. He stated, after my sister's death, and without consulting any of us surviving, that my mother had reared us in extreme Calvinism, and that certain Scottish Calvinist manuals had been familiar to us from earlier days. I instantly assured him that I had never in my life seen the books, and that my mother was far too wise a woman to train children to any sectarian religion. He did omit it in a second edition, but proceeded to imply that my mother had *come* to Oxford to *oppose* my brother! This, too, was wholly incorrect. My brother, with his great liberality, pressed my mother to change her abode and come *nearer to him;* I believe she dreaded to be a burden on him, and came reluctantly. The Rev. Th. Mozley also attributed my mother's "*Calvinism*" (of which I never heard or saw anything) to the fact that her *grandfather* had fled to England when the Edict of Nantes was revoked. Out of so small a matter may a wholly false *myth* grow! I now *infer* that my mother and sisters had opposed my brother's pretensions far more actively than I knew; for to me they were so reticent, that only after my mother's death did I learn that they were *not* his devotees.

I return to say, that the Rev. Mr. Snow, vicar of Richmond in Surrey, kindly read to me in the autumn of 1833 a letter from J. H. N., and his reply. He had no personal knowledge of my brother, and was much superior in age. The letter urged him *to claim* higher rights and powers as a clergyman. Mr. Snow's reply had two main paragraphs: First, he *regretted* that the clergy had not more moral weight in society, and he earnestly hoped for more. But, *they must earn it* by superiority in every form of goodness. After their past evil history, to *claim more power would bring on them keener contempt from men and heavier judgment from God* (the words still ring in my ears).

In my present abode I regained acquaintance with the late Rev. Charles Girdlestone, into whose Balliol Fellowship I succeeded in 1826. He kindly put into my hands the document sent to him (with a letter of November 1, 1833) by my brother, and his own reply. The document which my brother was actively circulating, he hereby adopted as his own, and probably drew it up as originally penned. Abridged of what the reader will himself supply, it speaks thus :—

"Events have occurred calculated to inspire the true members and friends of the Church with the deepest uneasiness. The privilege (a) possessed by parties hostile to her doctrine, ritual, and polity, of legislating for her, their avowed and unceasing efforts (b) against her, their alliance with such as openly reject (c) the Christian faith, and the lax and unsound principles of many (d) who profess and even think themselves her friends, these things have displayed themselves, &c. . . . . . Everyone who has become acquainted with the literature of the day must have observed the attempts made to reconcile members of the Church to alterations in its doctrine and discipline. Projects for the annihilation of our creeds and *the removal of doctrinal state-*

ments *incidentally contained* in our worship have been put forth. Our services have been subjected to a licentious criticism. Our apostolic polity has been ridiculed and denied. . . . . The spirit of the age is disposed to regard points of religious belief with indifference, and to sacrifice the interests of truth to notions of temporary convenience," &c. &c.

If there were not partial truths here, the document would not be plausible. It is not to the purpose here to analyse it minutely, but short remarks are appropriate.

(*a*) No special *privilege* is granted by Lord Grey to Nonconformists. Simply, *if they elect* a Nonconformist M.P., and a measure come before Parliament concerning a Church matter, he may vote on it, as one man out of more than 600, and with the contingency of a veto from the Lords.

(*b*) Unceasing efforts (of Dissenters) against the Church! The *worst* that any Dissenter had urged was mere separation of Church and State. This was precisely the thing which J. H. N. tells us that he himself and all the Tractarian party desired; yet here he "sacrifices the interest of truth to notions of temporary convenience," earnestly attacking those who happened to hold exactly his own sentiment. Dissenters had not claimed Church Property.

(c) He accuses Dissenters as *making alliance* with rejectors of Christian faith. Surely he means *alliance* to be understood as Church Alliance; if so, it seems to me a slander. If it means alliance of citizen with citizen for some civil good, can he possibly be so fanatical as to censure it?

(d) By the word *many* one may guess that he means Liberal statesmen who have tried to relieve Dissenters' grievances, or Evangelical grievances. But the delusion is in calling others than himself *unsound*, and hostile to the Church, while he himself is more hostile than any Whig statesman or any of the Nonconformists whom he calls hostile; and *is fully conscious that he hates the fundamental principle* of Private Judgment, which, in separating from Rome, the Anglican Church assumed.

The chief part of his private letter is as follows:—

"*Nov. 1st*, 1833.

"DEAR GIRDLESTONE,

"We are in motion from the Isle of Wight to Durham, and from Cornwall to Kent. Surely the Church will be shortly *delivered from the captivity under wicked men, who are worse than Chushan-rishathaim or the Philistines.* We groan under that heterogeneous, *un*-ecclesiastical Parliament, [here he distinctly echoes the Nonconformists] and *will not submit* to its dictation. We shall be truly glad of your co-operation, as of one who really fears God and wishes to serve Him; but if you will not, *we will march past you.*

"Yours,
"J. H. NEWMAN."

Mr. C. Girdlestone (his senior by four years) answers kindly, but says the document

"Breathes a censorious, querulous, discontented, defiant spirit likely to bring the Church into contempt, and opposite to the Christian rule of overcoming evil with good. I regard the men in power as no worse Christians than their (Tory) predecessors."

For which he gives illustration, and insists that the Church ought to show politically the same zeal, and the same self-denial, humility, and charity as in private life. He proceeds:

"Dear Newman, do not march past me as you threaten, lest you afterwards wish to march back again.

"Ever yours,
"C. GIRDLESTONE."

In 1827, the Rev. C. Girdlestone was a High Churchman, but my brother's career made him an Evangelical, as I understood him.

My last topic is a prelude to a far grander, which I call

THE HAMPDEN BUBBLE.

Mischievous and vexatious as the Bubble was, it was the greatest deed of Puseyism, the greatest and most manifest failure. Men younger than sixty can seldom know any of the details of this affair, and yet all ought to know at least the outlines.

The Rev. Renn Dickson Hampden had carried off literary honours so many as are hard to remember. He was a Fellow of Oriel before his marriage. As a country clergyman he produced a learned work that was thought a fit companion to Bishop Butler's "Analogy," as a bulwark to Christianity. In 1832 he preached the Bampton Lectures at Oxford with applause, apparently universal. In 1834 he became Professor of Whyte's Political Economy, to which he was elected by the University Vice-Chancellor, the Dean of Christchurch, the Presidents of Magdalen and St. John's, and the two Proctors. Oxford seemed to set its seal on his various accomplishments: his birth-year was 1793.

Lord Melbourne, whose principle was, *to please the Clergy, if he could*, appointed Dr. Hampden in February, 1836, to be Regius Professor of Divinity in Oxford. But my brother with all speed published a tract called "Elucidations" of Dr. Hampden, which, like a pebble flung into a lake, convulsed the whole area of Puseyism. No wonder, for when I read the pamphlet, it at once set *me* against Hampden, though I was an outsider and of course quiescent. His opponents gave notice of a movement in *Convocation* to prohibit attendance of University students on Dr. Hampden's lectures. This "Convocation" consists of all Masters of Arts, *lay or clerical*, who, by paying the annual fee, keep their names on the University Register. Every Puseyite Master of Arts was stirred to travel up to Oxford and vote. Probably from other parts came supporters to Hampden, but the most notable centre was Rugby, where Arnold opened the case to all his masters. They all (I understood) came with him to vote against the threatened measure. I had the details from Algernon

Grenfell, my old friend and co-equal as an undergraduate, who was then one of the Rugby masters.

As Dr. Arnold put the case : (1) We, when assembled in Convocation, are not judges of heresy, but are collectively mere laymen. It is superfluous to us to know, whether the Professor now appointed, deserves, or does not deserve, the stigma cast upon him. (2) But next, if we were the fit tribunal, common sense, common justice, and, I need not say, University Law, demand that an accused person shall have his fault defined,—in what page, paragraph, or line of his book has he offended. Now, Dr. Hampden cannot explain, cannot defend himself, cannot confess and retract. To forbid pupils to attend him, is to punish him in the dark, which is abominable. (3) Such an insurrection against the power of the Crown is rash and headlong. Only extreme necessity can justify it. We might bring the University into unknown and formidable danger.

"We (said Grenfell) agreed that our duty was simply to vote against the *Tribunal* and the *Process*, and not to touch the question of Heresy or no heresy." He was a personal friend of Keble's. He had lived in Keble's house—perhaps as a pupil—he had read in manuscript Keble's hymns (entitled "The Christian Year"), and he recited to me what was his last sight of Keble: "I had come up to Oxford with the Rugby band, and had voted against the proposed disabling of Hampden, when, walking in the High Street, I saw Keble on the opposite side, so I crossed hastily to clasp his hand. But he held his hand out of my reach, and, glaring on me, said solemnly: 'Grenfell! you have sacrificed at the altar of Jupiter, and I renounce your friendship from this day.'" After that tale, I doubted whether my friend found the loss of Keble's friendship very severe.

Such *fierce and blind fanaticism* had my brother's " Elucidations " spread far and wide! Dr. Hawkins, Provost of Oriel, had from the beginning defended Hampden as *not* having violated clerical right to speak freely on Church *History*. Probably few took the trouble to read Hampden's book, and when it was once keenly attacked, each dreaded to step into a pool where he might be out of his depth. But Hawkins was chivalrous, and so were a few others.

The measure in Convocation was carried against Hampden, whom it affected piteously. He seemed to have a host of bitter enemies, and very few defenders; and the reverse from long untainted honour to sudden contumely was to him dreadful. Baden Powell (present in the thick of it) declared to me that Hampden was too meek, and this, by the Puseyites, of whom few had read his book, was invariably interpreted as a sign of guilt. If he had shown *indignation* instead of mere *grief*, they might have understood that they were attacking an innocent man. His intellect was presently disparaged, as well as his orthodoxy, in the Oxford press; but this hardly deserves mention.

From Charles Knight's Biographical Dictionary I learn that the literature poured out in this controversy of eleven years was vast. I merely read the "Elucidations," and, many years later, Archdeacon Julius Hare's Review; thence first getting any clear idea how an able man, elected by the Crown to be Divinity Professor, could have run into Heresy *judged* so flagrant. The title to Hampden's lectures was "The Scholastic Philosophy in its relations to Church Theology." Julius Hare severely censured my brother, and I began to understand the inevitable discord between him and Hampden. The latter wished to separate scholastic additions from Church Theology and teach us to look back to earlier centuries for sounder knowledge of primitive truth. But with J. H. Newman the scholastic *additions* were the most valuable part, namely, that which he oddly called *tradition*. To give weight to the earlier fathers, and to depreciate as " scholastic " some of the later ones, seemed to my brother as rushing towards Arianism. I suppose he soon accepted as his *mission* " to crush Hampden."

Lord Melbourne's fixed alarm of " burning his fingers " with the Church, made the Hampden Nemesis linger until after the Irish Potato Famine. Sir Robert Peel resigned office, and Lord John Russell became Premier in 1847, who on the earliest opportunity chose Hampden for Bishop of Hereford. J. H. N. was no longer among Anglicans. Pusey, I think, had had to defend himself against some charge of Romish heresy. But younger Puseyites resolved with Keble to make a new trial of strength against the State.

As they had beaten Lord Melbourne, why should they think Lord John formidable? The Dean of Hereford, Dr. Merewether, was cordially with them. To cut matters short, a solemn deputation, with Keble at the head, was to be received in Oxford by the Bishop (Samuel Wilberforce) to protest against, and, so to say, bar out Dr. Hampden from Hereford. A Bishop has no palace in Oxford. Wilberforce received a night's hospitality from his ancient tutor, Dr. Hawkins, who for many years had continued Provost of Oriel. Next morning the Bishop presented himself to Keble and the deputation; but, I believe, before Keble could begin a long prepared and *awful* speech, a short utterance discomfited them all: "I now find that Dr. Hampden is faultless."

Thus the *Hampden bubble burst* suddenly.

Probably no reporter was in time to hear the explosion. Newspaper editors were as confounded as the general public. A report went forth with the following colour:—

"The Bishop of Oxford agreed to receive Mr. Keble's deputation on a near day. But before the day the Bishop learned, no doubt, that to oppose an appointment of the Crown could not be approved by the Court, nor by the Bishop's peculiar friend, H.R.H. the Prince Consort. Naturally therefore he thought it wiser to go no further in the matter."

Some say that from this affair the Bishop earned the title "Soapy Sam," with the amusing addition that when a little child asked, " Why do people call you Soapy Sam?" he answered, with the gracious readiness native to a Wilberforce, "Really, my little dear, I do not exactly know, but perhaps they mean that I take such pains to keep my hands clean."

In my belief this very clever Bishop never did an honester and braver deed than his acquittal of Hampden. Any pressure from the Court is quite a false idea. By strange accident I am able to publish the genuine story.

My old friend, the late Bonamy Price, well known in recent Oxford, had been a Rugby master, and with Grenfell and the rest had voted against disabling Hampden. Happening to be in Oxford just after the *Bubble* burst, he called on Dr. Hawkins, who had been gracious to him in old days; and inevitably the two began mutual congratulation on the event (I conjecture that the very fact led Bonamy to call on the veteran Provost). Hawkins was delighted and boiling over, and soon poured out very ample details of what passed between him and the Bishop.

After the Bishop perceived that his old tutor looked grave on the open war against Crown Patronage, and on the rumour that the Dean of Hereford would risk a Præmunire, the Bishop said, that to listen to Keble was not a new or active deed: that, in fact, he was constrained to it by consistency; for he had voted against Hampden's becoming Regius Professor of Divinity, and he could not possibly make light of unsoundness concerning such a doctrine as the Trinity. (These two points were the *fulcra* of the talk.) On the former, the Provost said: "You voted in 1836, true; but then you were a Curate; then, you were one out of four hundred; now, you are a Lord Bishop; then, your responsibility was *nil*; now, you will bring on yourself the chief responsibility. An error here may affect all your future life." When the Bishop made some remark that for sacred truth we must encounter great risk, he so expressed himself that

Hawkins exclaimed: "Bless me! why, you cannot have read Hampden's lectures; you can only have read Newman's elucidation of them." The Bishop replied: "Well, I must confess I could not for a moment distrust Newman." "Ah! my Lord, I do not blame you; four hundred trusted him, and I have no right to say, believe me rather than him. But since you have not read Hampden yourself, and must now, as Bishop, seem to judge his book, and to oppose his appointment by the Crown, I do say, that if you are a wise Bishop you will read his book *at once*. And I will tell you what! We ought this evening to sit side by side, and read the book together."

The Bishop freely confessed the wisdom of the advice, and acted on it. The two sat together, *with feet on fender* (the phrase stuck in my memory and I now find it was December) and read the lectures through from end to end.

Then the Bishop said, "My kind old tutor, you are right. I have no right to open my lips against Hampden."

What actual words the Bishop next day used to Keble I am not sure that I learned from Bonamy, but either from him or from some other quarter I heard them to be : "*I have now read Hampden myself*, and cannot presume to blame him." Apparently he *must* have told them this fact, and in one newspaper a cry of *indignation* arose that he ever had condemned Hampden without reading his book.

CHAPTER IV.

DECLINE AND FALL.

OF all the deeds performed collectively by those called Puseyites, the most signal was the attack on Dr. Hampden, and most signal was its failure. Of this deed the main responsibility fell on my brother by his tract called " Elucidations."

If a reader objects that he declines to accept my account of Bishop Wilberforce having read Hampden's lectures *in private*, and that after all the Bishop had no power to *acquit*, the obvious and sufficient reply is, that there had been no previous tribunal, and no count of accusation formulated. The iniquity of the proceeding is carried back to that against which the band from Rugby protested. The Masters of Arts in Convocation had no jurisdiction over religious error; not one out of twenty would have thought himself a competent judge; and their *silencing* of Hampden without notifying what had been his offence is so clear, that, but for the base excuse of fanaticism and *trust in Rev. J. H. N.*, one might use much stronger epithets. Eleven years, 1836-1847, passed before the bubble burst. Then I began to understand how dark a stain it branded on my brother's Christian character.

He had specially studied the history of those mournful times in which men called Christians turned Christianity into " doubtful disputations" concerning the Triple Divine Essence, and decided their contests either by the bludgeons of monks or by the swords of imperial soldiers. Had he never learned that " the kingdom of God is not" intellectual precision in things *superhuman*, τα δαιμόνια of Socrates, " but righteousness, peace, and spiritual joy"?

The *Christian sentiment* makes, and *nothing else makes* the true Christian. That intellectual error on a tangled and obscure subject may happen to any pious and good man, is so obvious that one asks, had J. H. N. never suspected that Hampden, his elder, and *by far more highly honoured*, might be *more* correct *than* he concerning the scholastic modifications of the Trinity? He had personal knowledge of the imputation of *heresy*, which Whately (afterwards Archbishop) incurred by a well-meant attempt to reconcile the Trinity with logic; and how unfairly a priest is damaged by such imputation. Not even a layman can often afford to laugh at it. A clergyman may be half ruined by it.

J. H. N. cannot have been unaware that *to defend* a clergyman accused of heresy in these controversies is so dangerous to the defender himself that timid priests stand aloof. If Hampden had written something that seemed to J. H. N. doubtful or unwise, at least one might have hoped that the younger would address a friendly note to the elder, craving a secret talk. Instead of this, he rushed into hostility, and that, according to Archdeacon Julius Hare, and others, with inaccuracy so strong and so clever as to excite disapproval apparently beyond their utterance. My brother was thirty-five when he wrote those "Elucidations." He knew that he was the real head of a religious party, through whom he hoped to regenerate England. Did this inspire modesty and caution? Was there any mark of Christian tenderness or just humility? Rather it seemed that incipient Power goaded him at once into rash precipitation and recklessness of justice. I fully believe that my brother was unconscious of injustice. It did not occur to him that he might have something himself *to learn*, as well as to *teach*, but the grievous fact is, that he had no practical humility or tenderness, and did not remember, when he had 400 troops ready to obey him, that this did not give him spiritual, but only Pagan force; moreover, that since he had condescended to receive Holy Orders in the Anglican Church, then without some very flagrant iniquity on the part of the Crown officials, Crown patronage must not be treated with contempt and defiance. The grave impropriety of his conduct enlarges on closer view. In short, he so used his "private judgment" as (in appearance) to say to his Brother Priest, MOREH, "Thou rebel!" The Jesus[*] who uttered fierce doom on this offence was at least no Heresy-hunter.

Seldom and short as were my visits to

---

[*] Matt. v. 22.

Oxford in those days, I always heard of some whimsical utterance from St. Mary's pulpit, difficult to invent, and ingenious. Nothing like it was told concerning others of my brother's party, and the reports were believed by persons whom I respected. I may mention two as specimens.

First, as to Church buildings, J. H. N. was quoted thus :—" I by no means blame the building of a church where it is wanted for human use ; on the contrary, I greatly commend it. But it cannot compete in merit with a sacred building *not* wanted by men and women ; for in the latter case it is built for the honour and glory of God, which is a much higher end of action than the convenience or services of men. And if, in the church erected for God, many empty seats be observed, this fact ought not to discourage us ; for if they are empty of human sitters, yet undoubtedly in every seat apparently empty an angel of God is sitting."

Next I heard how J. H. N. applied Aristotle's doctrine of Habit to Christian service. The Greek philosopher assumes mankind as in general having not only a conscience reproving them when they choose the worse rather than the better, but that men do on the whole approve virtue more than vice, therefore are amenable to moral teaching. He vehemently dissents from Socrates, who thought Knowledge to be the whole difference of a good from a bad man. Preference of goodness is the cardinal point, which Socrates did not see. Aristotle is painfully aware that men are often so depraved as to prefer vice to virtue, and thus become inaccessible to teaching (ἀνίατοι, incurable). Such a one needs training. He is (as we say) unprincipled: Οὐκ ἔχει τὰς ἀρχάς, he has not the First Principles. What does training mean? The incurable man or child must be set to practise *good deeds*, and, though he has as yet no heart for goodness, yet little by little he may gain or recover it. We at once see that a total change of *surroundings* is what Aristotle prescribed, and *we* add, *loving faces*. But my brother's alleged application of this doctrine sounds very novel. For " practice of *good deeds* " he substituted " practice of *Church ceremonies*," and, after other argument, summed up with, " Thus we repeat the Creeds in Church, *not because* we believe them, but *in order* that we may believe them." Was it my duty to despise this, as only a clever joke? But the doctrine of Sacred Habit at once explained my brother's eagerness to set "The Blessed Virgin," upon my wall, as the old Greek said ἐκ τοῦ ὁρᾶν τὸ ἐρᾶν (From sight comes love). I have since learned that Catholics think themselves *persecuted* by our new National Education, because their children are not allowed pictures of their saints in the public schools. Moreover, elder Oxonians remember the scandal caused when it was published that Keble had advised Arnold to put down his doubts on the Trinity by main force, and *take a curacy to get rid of them;* which implied that Keble equally clung to this doctrine of Sacred Habit. Further, another strange affair seemed that it was rightly ascribed to my brother. I do not know that my brother Charles ever was in Oxford, nor can have heard Oxford gossip, yet he repeated to me as of John's address to him, not only the same doctrine, but a still more extravagant application of it as "treatment for Atheism!" I wrote down his narrative, but it is so ludicrous that I may be thought to invent it, and the whole is really superfluous. Until this brother's character developed itself, I never understood that of a Greek Diogenes, only lacking his hardihood and impudence.

I now draw the curtain over my brother Charles, and mention the last words concerning him which I remember from my sister Harriet: " Charles is a sore thorn to us : but oh ! how much sorer would it be, if he were a rogue or a profligate."

The formula, " We recite the Creed not because we believe it, but in order that we may believe it," seems cleverly to put into a nutshell the history of national creeds, as they grow up under a wholly uncritical people—the Barbaric method, careless of truth, which in Romanist Missions, as far as I have read, seems to be adopted *on system* with the purpose of raising, *in the next generation* at least, an obedient uncritical flock. To represent uncritical barbarism as the fit wisdom of an aspiring people, was only the perverse form of *bravery* which dazzled the very critical and poetical John Henry Newman.

Probably about 1840 I fell into a delusion

which I have only recently discovered. I thought I read in an Oxford paper a frank avowal of my brother:

"I have been teaching *Roman* doctrine in Oxford, lest Anglicans go to Rome to get it."

The frank avowal of what I had known since 1833 to be true, seemed to me like becoming an honest man, and I thought, "Better late than never," and it gladdened me. But criticism by others now teaches me that there was some mistake either in the newspaper or in my interpretation. Some tell me that he must have written:

"I have been teaching *Catholic* doctrine in Oxford, lest Anglicans go to Rome to get *Papal*" [*else*, to get *Roman*].

And this example excellently shows the advantage with which his use of the three epithets could enable him to play his own game on simpler minds. His two hymns, which I produce (pp. 56, 58), were not strictly Papal, for there is no mention of a Pope, and I well believe that the Pope was the last element of Romanism that he admitted. Also other English priests wish to hold priestly power themselves, but do not relish a Pope riding on their own shoulders. But if you convert anyone to the doctrine of the two hymns, a priest in England implies a Pope only geographically or politically differing.

It is better to pass very slightly over years concerning which others know more than I, perhaps 1838 and 1839. I just remember that a Mr. Ward, of Balliol, excited disgust by claiming as legitimate (what he called) a *non-natural* sense of test articles, and I think out of this rose the celebrated Tract XC. I was so sick of the whole subject, that I never took the trouble of getting the tract to read. I was also preoccupied with my own literary work and my own religious inquiries. But four Oxford students, of whom one was afterwards known as Tait, first as Bishop of London, next as Archbishop of Canterbury, made public protest against the (anonymous?) Tract XC., which led to the first visible check to my brother's career. Many elder men had entirely disapproved it from the beginning, but thought it more prudent to let the rush of fanaticism disclose its weakness before assailing it. Arnold compared its opponents to ships caught in a tornado, whose wisdom is to cast all their anchors firmly and wait till the fierceness of the gale is spent. The then Bishop of Oxford in the gentlest way put to trial my brother's obedience to his bishop, by indicating that the Tracts ought not to be continued. All the rigmarole of non-naturalism was "bored through its castle wall by a little pin"! but this part of the Epic is too difficult for me.

I cannot be sure of the year, perhaps it was 1842, that I went to Rugby to visit my college friend Bonamy Price, who eagerly asked me, "Have you seen that extraordinary Confession to a Priest in an Oxford Newspaper?" I had not. He produced it. It was elaborate, in many paragraphs, and defined, with contrition, past literary sins. It had no signature, and no explanation *why* it was inserted (as an advertisement). The sins confessed were words derogatory to the Papacy, and one paragraph quoted the sinful words written " in *my* history of the Arians." This at once showed that the penitent writer meant my brother. Then, why was not his name signed to it? We had guesses about that. One guess was that his confessor had violated secrecy. Another, more probable, that a priest had written it out in his own phraseology, had presented it to my brother to sign, but could not extort his signature : they had put it in without the signature, though with the words "*my* history of the Arians," defying my brother to prosecute him, and hoping thus to cut off his retreat from Rome.

Unless my brother had been able to say to a jury, " The whole thing has been done without my cognizance and against my will and has cunningly evaded forging my name, which they are aiming to extort, but never shall," a jury would give only nominal damages. The Church of Rome could afford to run that risk. Meanwhile the public was certain to infer that my brother had long had dealings with a Romish priest, and had made so weak resistance as to encourage him to *coercion*. Coercion it seemed to be. If the slippery victim refused to submit, he retired from the contest damaged in reputation.

What was the truth as to this half-and-half publication is an enigma. The Church of Rome must know all about it. But if it involved a cunning *coercion*, they are not likely to proclaim that they outwitted and captured the man whom they have been so signally honouring.

My brother prudently and wisely withdrew from preaching for about three years (1842, 3, 4 ?) I *think*. Already in 1841 the tide had turned against him, because of his peculiar pupils going over to the Papacy. He took at Littlemore three continuous cottages as a sort of monastery for himself and some others. In my visit I found the atmosphere of Oxford most hostile to him. In the shops were caricatures and cartoons, with guideposts to show the way to Rome. The newspapers had *bitter* complaints from parents, who had believed that he had a special *via media* to save their sons from Rome, and, lo! it had led them thither. The general sentiment proclaimed him to be a wolf in sheep's clothing. The city seemed to cry to him, " Get out ! " and his pupils from Rome to cry, " You are bound in honesty to come after us." This double pressure needed a total renunciation of his twenty years' preaching, unless he would yield, as he did yield.

When I met him, his deportment to me was

greatly changed. He had come down from his high horse. I thought that first his humiliation about Tract XC. might have done him good; but now far greater was the manifest contempt and aversion of the public. I frankly told him Rome was his only fit place: he did not resent it. People told me of the unnatural self-torments of the supposed monks in his Littlemore retreat. I remember only that of coming out of a warm bed by night, and standing with naked feet on a cold hearthstone. *It may have been invention;* but it recalled to my mind Blanco White's prediction as to what he was driving into—*before* his Ordination.

And now the endeavour is made to falsify history; I suppose by men *quite too young to remember it.* Thackeray in "Pendennis" makes his speaker say whatever is convenient, and declares that my brother, in leaving the Anglican Church, "gave up friends, fame, *dearest ties, closest vanities* [is this a strange misprint?], the respect of an army of churchmen, the recognised position of a leader, and passes over (truth impelled) to the enemy." Thackeray was not writing history; but

Mr. G. W. Foote, a fine writer, editor of the *Freethinker*, and an avowed atheist, on August 17 this year writes: "Thackeray was not exaggerating," and so, I find, young people believe. But it is just the opposite of truth. *Fame: the respect of an army of churchmen; the recognised position of a leader:* these were lost and irrecoverable, when facts had proved that his doctrine was full-blown Romanism, garnished with the pretence that Anglicanism had no essential difference from Romanism. But our chief atheistic[*] organ very zealously took his part against Kingsley, and Mr. G. W. Foote now extols him for teaching that *there is no logical standing-place between Rome and Atheism.*

It is pleasanter to argue against an Atheist than against the late Cardinal, who gained everything by joining those whom he ought to have joined twelve years earlier. By staying in the wrong camp he incurred taunts and execration. Among Romanists he gained a

---

[*] I so call the *Westminster Review*, because Dr. James Martineau declined to continue writing for it, *because* it interpolated atheistical articles between his theistic articles.

home and dignified retreat, in which he lived happily for forty-six years; and when he no longer was a traitor in our camp he became an honourable foe. Protestants ceased to fear him, and saw all his best side. The report of his private virtues seems quite to have endeared him to the people of Birmingham. In the Oratory he attained a tranquillity and a position of honour simply impossible to him until he moved into his rightful place.

But I have words of personal defence against Mr. G. W. Foote. He says that *I am constrained to admit* that the proofs of God's existence are not what I once thought them. He does not say *what* nor *where*, and I simply wonder. On the contrary, I have never ceased to regard Atheism as monstrous folly, and more than ever since in the last thirty years " a *self-acting* Universe " is talked of. Concerning a Future Life, I hold the same conviction as I heard and approved of in Oxford sixty-five years ago, that *without Supernatural Revelation* it can only be a (pious) *opinion*, not a *doctrine*. I still so believe, and have maintained it against the Rev. Charles Voysey. Then he infers that I do not judge *according to Evidence*, because I "regard some forms of Theism as *essential* to human morality and *elevation*." I do not think he has my words correctly, but I insist that *I do judge according to Evidence:* first, that our Creator exists; next, that he has given to each of us a Will capable of *sinning* (that is, of thwarting his purposes); and thirdly, that he is *observant* of our conduct. This is my Theism: such it was from childhood. Then I received these without Evidence: long ago, I seem to have adequate proof. I know further; that some believe in a Creator, but cannot attain a belief that he deigns to notice our conduct, good or bad. I do not think the Theism of these can at all animate their morality. I know that my Theism does animate the morality of all who hold it. How does that imply that I believe it *without Evidence?* Mr. G. W. Foote has something to learn.

No wonder he is delighted with the late Cardinal,—if his quotations are correct. He tells us that the Cardinal dreaded Atheism, but *never argued against it: he knew that that was hopeless.* (Is that a fact? I am not *up* in the Grammar of Assent, some readers may perhaps correct Mr. Foote's fact.) But, if the Cardinal avowed that it was hopeless to argue against Atheists, that may merely mean that they are lower than ordinary normal mankind and he treats them with contempt. But others will defend the Cardinal on this head. What, also, of his avowal that there is no logical standing-point *between* Romanism and Atheism, but whatever is between is gliding down into Atheism? Delightful news! Since the days of Isaiah and Micah have the whole Jewish nation been so gliding? If the Cardinal so read History, it is a merit to Atheists. I do *not* so read History in Europe, nor in Asia.

Mr. Foote tells us that the Cardinal could not rest without " *certitude,*" and that was only to be had in Rome. If he mean that the Cardinal *ever* thought the existence of God our Creator was uncertain, or that greater certitude was afforded by entering the Roman Church, I think Mr. Foote must be wrong in fact. But, if by " certitude " he mean a better knowledge of how many Persons coexisted in one God, in short, certitude concerning the inner essence and constitution of Godhead, it is marvellous to me how this can seem commendable to an Atheist. I do not tax the Cardinal with this sentiment. But if anyone say, "I cannot be happy without *certitude* on such divine secrets," and I *get* certitude by using my private judgment to pass from one Church to another, I should rather expect a man who stands up for evidence as does Mr. Foote to say, "This is as silly as in a child to cry for the moon, and say, 'I shall never be happy till I get it.'" I should myself add : the second infatuation is still less *logical*, to think to evade error by a voluntary adoption of a new Creed and Church. Mr. Foote also has no right to say that there is no *logical* standing-place *between* the Roman Creed and Atheism, unless he uphold the Roman Creed as itself *logical*. Can we believe that Mr. Foote looks on the Nicene Creed, and the Creed falsely called Athanasian, with its Three Divine Persons who are *not* Three Gods, as eminently *logical?* Unless he does, he is writing *not* sincerely, *not* truthfully, but to support his own foolish Atheism. As for me, he fancies that my faith (he says) is *crumbling* away, because I try to retain only what is best, truest, noblest in Hebrew and Christian faith. To me it is undeniable fact (of which we have nothing to boast) that we are, as we ought to be, wiser than the ancients. We mount on their shoulders, and have means of avoiding error which they had not. We look out on a far broader world than did ancient teachers for whom we thank God; but to hamper ourselves by the errors *incident to their age* is a folly and almost a sin. I tell Mr. Foote that my faith, my hopes, my joy keep rising, as I see Christian sects vying in *good works*, and of late even Catholics joining with Protestants. This is the way to improve the world, and to improve one another. As initiator of this grand movement, I with delight signalize Cardinal Manning, though happily he is not at all alone among Catholics. The Evangelicals, whom my brother so unhappily despised, seem, with Quakers, Unitarians, and others, doing a work which will change the aspect of the world. We are in the beginning only. The awakening of Womanhood is the dawn of a new era, equivalent to the making Christian purity the goal of our civilization.

CHAPTER V.

CONTRAST OF TWO CARDINALS.—THE "APOLOGIA."

But this new movement of Christians leads me on to another painful phenomenon in the late Cardinal's character.

On October 22nd, 1867, Archbishop Manning made his first appearance in the Free Trade Hall, Manchester, to co-operate with Protestants against the enormous excess of the trade in Intoxicating Drink. For a year previous he had investigated the subject, and had taken the precaution to discuss the matter at headquarters, so as to act without fear of higher disapproval. I was on the platform and heard him with delight. The vast audience felt as one heart and one soul. We knew what sacrifice of time and energy a man of onerous duties and great influence has to make, when he breaks through routine in the cause of fundamental *public morality*, and makes speeches which must incur certainly much criticism, probably much ill-will, besides the novelty of standing on a common platform with Protestants. It filled me with enthusiasm and joy, but I was merely a type of the thousands who listened in deep rapt silence to his magnificent speech. I wrote at once to my brother, believing that I had got a topic on which we should at length find *interest in common*. I cannot guarantee my words, but I know that I was elated and my admiration warm. He replied in a kind note, but with only these few words bearing on my topic : " As to what you tell me of Archbishop Manning, I have heard that some also of our Irish bishops think that too many drink-shops are licensed. As for me, I do not know whether we have too many or too few."

This seemed to curdle my heart like a lump of ice. I handed the note to a Manchester friend, who exclaimed : " Why ! one would think he was living on a different planet." [Since writing this I learn from a passage in the " Apologia " (p. 112) that his writing in the *Record* Newspaper was stopt by the editor when he wanted *to attack Temperance Societies* (about 1834).]

I knew not how to believe the truthfulness of his ignorance. It was more like to the ignorance affected by Socrates to get advantage in an argument than to Christian simplicity. But, to try whether my expectation had been unreasonable, I wrote *for* J. H. N. an *imaginary* reply, which ran thus:—

> "I do indeed rejoice that at last we have a wish in common, and better still, that not I and you only, but Catholics and Protestants are beginning to co-operate for the public morality, which is older than any religion and a main purpose for which religion ought to exist. I have not myself had leisure to look into the statistics of licensing; but my revered Archbishop has the mind of a statesman, and, I am fully persuaded, knows well all needful details. I know also that some at least of our Irish bishops hold the same view. Nay, I remember that Father Theobald Mathew was so honoured for his exertions in this same cause, that many expected him to be canonised as a Saint. I cannot err in the broad statement that intoxicating drink is a main and cruel factor of violent crime, of misery to wives, pauperism, and hideous impurity. Be sure that you all and the Archbishop carry my heart warmly with your joint efforts."

I could not see that I had set down a word more than I had *a right to expect;* but further study opened a new thought: Has he not some *difference* which makes him cold to the Archbishop? But I trampled the thought down, saying: Any possible difference must be very small compared to what I and the thousands of our U.K.A. Protestants have with every Romanist; yet, with us all, the joy of co-operation in a holy cause swallows up our difference. The more I dwelt on this icy message, the less it seemed worthy, not only of a Christian, but of one who cared for human sin and human misery. I could not forget what fierce anger he had avowed when Irish bishoprics had been suppressed on the ground that they had no flocks needing them (I think this was the reason). To *that* Anger contrast this Apathy. The year 1869 suddenly laid open to us the infamous C. D. Acts, supported by *each Cabinet in turn*, with the medicals, the military and naval authorities. Cardinal Manning nobly stood out against that also from the first; also since against Scientific Torture; later, how valuable has been his arbitration in strikes! He was seven years younger than my brother. But from forty-seven years among the Catholics strike off the odd seven. In the forty years how grand, painfully grand in moral aspect, is the contrast of Manning, Archbishop and Cardinal! All men have not the same gifts, but all may sympathise in good works.

When my brother softened to me (a change which I ascribed to his humiliation from the discovery that his Via Media *against* Rome was carrying him captive *to* Rome) I tried to soften him to my sister Harriet also; but he silenced me by a decisive utterance: "Harriet has *that* in her *which I cannot permit.*" No doubt: she had keen common-sense and sisterly frankness, which he could not *permit*. She died after a long illness in 1852, and he never saw her again.

I now think that in justice to my brother I must tell what I had intended to hide, because I know it from my sister only; but it entirely harmonized with his Divine Mission hinted at in the "Apologia" (p. 99, &c.). He presented himself to my mother and sisters as a Divine Prophet, and, when repulsed, reproached my mother in the words: "No wonder; for the Scripture tells us that no prophet is without honour, save among his own people and in his father's house." I did not dare to press her with any further question which might have been painful to answer; but some other remarks of hers which I cannot tell to the public showed me that she had lost esteem for him from his conduct towards our mother (*other than* his inadmissible pretensions named above), and that she may have clashed with him more deeply than I know. To this also agrees that her husband (Rev. Th. Mozley) makes the strange mistake concerning my mother alluded to in p. 72. His little book displays him as a warm partizan of my brother, and (generous man as he is) he is as severe against Evangelicals as J. H. N. could wish. I darkly surmise painful collisions between my brother *on the one side* and my mother and elder sister *on the other*. My second sister was charming to everybody, and a type of unselfishness. On Harriet's death I wrote a fictitious epigram of epithets on her, and the first was, *Magnanimous*. She was not, like Jemima, charming to everybody; for to *some* she could speak disagreeable truths plainly. She *may* have offended J. H. N. by words sharper than we can guess.

In the Achilli case, I could not help thinking the verdict of the jury against him to be quite just.

The Hampden Bubble blew up in 1847, and could not raise my brother's repute. But when once he dropt false colours and avowed himself a Romanist, every year improved his moral position. However much we wonder when one trained in Protestantism changes to Romanism, still we all know that eminently good and a few eminently able men do so change. No one feels unkindly or judges harshly *if all is open and honourable.* General opinion silently and steadily was setting in in favour of my brother. He had only to leave his reputation to others, and not bring back a controversy twenty years old and more. Nevertheless, he wrote to me an unexpected letter, in a gayer tone than usual, to inform me that he should soon publish a book which would show some people his conduct in a new light. Probably he did not guess how painfully I had studied his two hymns since 1833, and that I had judged them inexcusable, indefensible from one presenting himself as an Anglican. Of course, I made no reply, only thought, " Who will now read the stale controversy ? " I do not know the exact year of this, *perhaps* 1862. But suddenly came from

Charles Kingsley words which my brother resented, and from Kingsley a sharp reply. Soon I saw that this quarrel might sell my brother's book; for he now could pose as a pious retired priest, *assailed* about old affairs belonging to a Church *which he had long left.* If he had wished for peace, he might have had it by a little meekness, not too much to expect in a Christian leader. He might have addressed Mr. Kingsley thus :

" Rev. Sir !—You are severe upon me : I am not surprized at it ; I do not blame you ; for I unwittingly caused sore grief to parents of my pupils. But I think you overlook a critical fact. A peer in the last century taunted your Church with having Calvinistic Articles, a Popish Liturgy, and an Arminian Clergy. This description is still true, and it involves a cruel and scandalous trap to ardent young men. You probably look on what you call its ' Protestant ' side as overwhelming everything, and you forgive your own neglects ; ought you to be quite so sharp on me, if my eyes were dazzled by its ' Popish ' side ? Claim that your formulas be made self-consistent, and perhaps it may make more evident to you that two honest men may see quite different faces in your Church as she is and has been.

"Yours, &c., J. H. N."

Some such reply, I believe, would have won from so generous a man as C. Kingsley a far more cordial and real apology, and would have raised my brother with us Protestants far more highly than did his quarrelsome rhetoric, so acceptable to the Atheists. His personal narrative perhaps would not have been less read; yet my "perhaps" is a miserably weak word. He seemed unable to understand the force of gentleness and modesty. His admirers tell me he was very *Christian*. My life has been a long sadness that I never could see it in him. His hymns of 1832 breathe contempt, defiance, and self-conceit. In his "Apologia" he does not see how ridiculous he makes both himself and Hurrell Froude by assuming as their motto the words of Homeric Achilles—

"Now that *I* am coming *back* to battle, you will feel the difference."

The narrative of his religious changes would have deeply interested me, but I suppose he was incapable of writing it. I turned with faint hope to learn *why* he passed over from Thomas Scott, of Aston Sandford, to a belief in Baptismal Regeneration; from sound New Testament Doctrine to magic; but the "Apologia" only tells me that he *learnt* it from Dr. Hawkins. And how came he to make prominent in his faith what the old Jews called " Blasphemy "—that a man can forgive Sin ? Nor only so, but that a chain of men for 1800 years have possessed this power, among whom were the ambitious and violent, the carnal and cruel, the ignorant and the fraudulent. The only reply of the "Apologia" is: "The Rev. William James *taught* me;" as if men's names ought to satisfy us, and reasons go for nothing. We want to know *why* he changed, not *who taught* him. At the same time, the change was simple and easy; he yielded to the Church Liturgy quickly after his ordination; which strongly suggests that not Argument but " Sacred Habit " was the converting power. To this agrees his apparent forgetfulness in the hymn against " Private Judgment," that *evidence* plays or ought to play any part in religious convictions.

In the "Apologia" I am sadly unable to believe that his reasons for leaving the Anglican Church are at all ingenuously told.

When the book came out, being accidentally introduced to a man among the very highest in Oxford, who also stands aloof from party, I said: "If it is not an improper question, may I ask whether those who knew Oxford while my brother was prominent think that he has fairly given in his 'Apologia' the true reasons of his leaving the Anglican Church?" "Oh!" answered he, "we could not expect it of him; of course he could not tell the real reasons to the public." I at once understood him. Neither could I expect J. H. N. to be over-candid. If he had said *nothing*, all would be right; but, as if to cover a retreat, he must forsooth go out with smoke and tramp and military music. His alleged reasons cannot have been written to be understood. One must first know whether St. Augustine or "the Donatists" were in the right, and what means Augustine's epigram " Securus judicat Orbis Terrarum." When appealed to as late Professor of Latin to interpret this, I could only reply: The word Securus has in good Latin two different senses: *originally,* reckless, careless; *secondarily,* secure, safe; just as with us " a harbour *reckless of* tempests" might pass over into " a harbour *safe against* tempests." So the epigram says—

<blockquote>
Either   The globe of the Earth is reckless in judgment.
Or   The globe of the Earth is safe in judgment.
</blockquote>

But neither yields to me intelligible sense.

Next: the Archbishop of Canterbury (dreadful thought!) made a compact with a Prussian (Lutheran-Calvinistic) minister about a bishop in Jerusalem. How possibly such a deed should make the Anglican Church unbearable is truly absurd; or what service it does here except to raise a cloud.

Since this MS. has been in the printer's hands the following has reached me in the last September number of the *Christian Irishman,* Dublin, concerning the late Cardinal:—

> "In 1842 he established an ascetic community in Littlemore. He soon saw that his influence with the mass of the English people was gone. He tells us himself that 'public confidence in him was at an end, and his occupation was gone.' He describes how he was himself posted up by the marshal on the butteryhatch of every College of his University after the manner of discommoned pastrycooks, and denounced in every class of society and in every organ of opinion as a

traitor who was caught in the act of firing his train against the time-honoured Establishment. This was the very thing to drive Newman into the Church of Rome, and *it did*."

I do not know from what writing of my brother the editor quotes; but he seems to have the book before him, and thus the Cardinal himself avows the *untruth* of Thackeray as quoted and justified by Mr. G. W. Foote above.

Finally, as regards my brother's devotion to the Virgin *after* he became a Romanist, the following scrap of newspaper has been given me :—

From a Sermon in Praise of the Virgin, by Dr. Newman, 1869 or '70 :—

"So intense was the Virgin's love of God, that it drew Him from heaven into her womb." Such is the *erotic, erratic, esoteric* utterance of the enthusiastic preacher.

CHAPTER VI.

ADDRESS TO PROTESTANTS.

I AM glad that I have said nearly my last word concerning the late Cardinal, and may now proceed to ask leave to address Protestants on certain causes of conversions to Rome, which so painfully dislocate families.

I. Against Romanists the chief weakness of Protestants turns on the variety of creeds to which the same " New Testament " leads them.

II. This discord is caused by the fact of the first Reformers adopting as sacred and fundamental truth an untenable tradition of the National Churches called Catholic.

III. When Protestants abandon this error they will gravitate towards unity and fixedness, as to the meaning of books held sacred.

I think my first thesis hardly needs argument, so evident is the fact.

But II., *without any other evidence but empty Catholic tradition*, Luther, Calvin, and Knox accepted the doctrine that our present N.T. is, verse by verse, divinely inspired, and has direct authority from God: except indeed that Luther was scornful of the Apocalypse, and looked askance at James's noble Epistle. But this eccentric position of Luther did not affect the general course of Reformed Doctrine.

From this Traditional Dogma followed the mischief which (as I have often tried to call attention) the works of John Wesley and even Bishop Butler would suffer, if a theory were accepted that every sentence from them was divinely guaranteed. The interpretation of their writings would at once be perverted. Every enigmatical, paradoxical, or unsound judgment would at once receive disproportionate attention and high authority. Their strong and wise side would be in comparison neglected; every error or fantasy would be mischievously aggrandised. What is best in them would be thought commonplace, and to believe whatever is weakest would be thought a high merit, *because* it mortifies our good sense. This very mischief was inflicted on the New Testament and grievously damaged the Reformation in the theories since named Calvinism, which in its most odious form were elicited by Calvin out of Paul of Tarsus. As David Hume sarcastically, yet truly said : " When men were asked to believe that God was an arbitrary tyrant they preferred to believe that he was a wafer." We now see clearly enough, how Calvin ought to have reasoned. In 1 Cor. xv., and in Romans, ch. xi., Paul seems to teach salvation for all who are to exist. In 1 Tim. ii. 4, " Who will have all men to be saved "; and iv. 10, he says, God is the Saviour of all men, *especially* of those who believe ; therefore Calvin cannot rightly press Paul's argument in Romans ix. Nor can he deny that one text contradicts the other ; *therefore* we must make allowance *for haste in writing,* and not take on ourselves to call every word which he writes to be guaranteed to us as the Word of God. We know that Apostles sometimes differed. Each accepted the other as a man divinely inspired, but that did not mean that he *never erred;* and why should written words be infallible, if spoken words are not ?

In Puritan New England Calvinism was intensely strong. Rev. W. Ellery Channing tells (rightly, I believe) how it broke down, not by new exposition and interpretation of Paul's argument, but by the strengthening of men's *good sense*. Hebrews and Christians alike had been accustomed to refute Pagan religion by pointing at cruelty and impurity imbedded in them: therefore they could not justly claim for their own creed exemption from like attack. If the Pagan could fairly impute arbitrary cruelty to the God in our creed, the fact would be an adequate refutation of our creed. So soon as men were bold enough to apply the same measure to their own creed as to foreign creeds, Calvinism was really doomed. Morality is older and higher than any special religion. Each religion in turn must stand before its tribunal. In the particular case of Calvinism it took the form: "Whatever avows God to be tyrannical cannot be true, whoever preaches it." Thus grew up in Christendom a stronger and nobler morality, dumbly uttering, "No Sacred Book shall blacken to me the face of God, whom I cannot worship if he be not far better than I am." What else would Calvin's Paul make of him but a more powerful Devil?

Calvinism is not quite dead, but it has died away wonderfully. In my boyhood Arminianism and Calvinism seemed the opposite flags of Protestants, as of Wesley and Whitfield. To which flag any active body belongs, for forty years back I seldom seem to hear. Now, what is herein implied? Men have *in this special case* learned that *it is our duty* to employ HUMAN MORALITY to criticise the Newer Scripture as well as the older. Paul, tent-maker, preacher, and traveller, was a very busy man. Whether he dictated a letter or wrote it, he must often have been in a great hurry. He quoted the older Scripture often by mere memory. Every learned critic knows that he is not always accurate. He never proposes his Epistles as A NEW SACRED LETTER, but writes in disparagement of tables of stone in contrast to the Law written in the heart. What *right* had Luther or Calvin to palm upon him a divine honour, destroy for him the excuse of hasty composition, and turn his small errors into a monstrous mischief? Go among the half-educated who look on every sentiment of Paul as divine, and dare not use their *good sense* against a single word : you will there find diverse interpretation at its maximum. *This* generates the discord which is our weakness. Go among more learned men who know the impossibility of stickling for verbal inspiration, and you find the discord dwindling, the errors of the Apostle largely imputed to weakness *incident to the age*, and high honour and reverence given to him for the eminence which raised him *above* his age. While criticism is arbitrarily crippled, you have necessarily *discord*, but free criticism ever moves towards *concord*. In the case of Paul that of the whole New Testament is typified.

In the Historical books—the Gospels and Acts—the case against Verbal Inspiration is stronger still, because even if each were written by one man, in no case does that one man claim to be an Apostle ; and the introduction to Luke makes pretension so modest, that we may say he no more claims inspiration than does Livy or Tacitus. To accept this tradition of verbal inspiration merely because in the close of the second century the Oligarchy of the Church adopted it as convenient in controversy, cannot be approved by any historian seeking after TRUTH; and while Christianity is presented as a historical religion, no treatment but the historical is just. Only Truth can unite us: but in seeking more complete truth, each individual and each sect must cease to nail down his or its *existing* creed as sacred; least of all, when it rests only on a tradition which has no valid support.

As colleges for Nonconformists have risen, and as fetters have one by one been struck off from the Old Universities, learning has softened down asperities. I know that a talk of *Down-Grade* has given alarm. Let those who raise the cry take their Reformation from the first century, not from the sixteenth; else, whatever their present honour, it will have no honour, but rather ignominy, in the light of fundamental search, which must come upon the *Origines Christianæ*. [Since the above was with the printer, I rejoice to read that in the National Protestant Congress the *first* century, not the *fourth*, is claimed as the starting-point.]

About the year 1820 three great names were prominent in Oxford: Davison, Copleston,

Whately. Of these Davison, no longer resident in 1824, was esteemed the highest. I read a volume of his sermons with great instruction. I do not remember the title, but the subject was the *gradual* revelation which God has made of himself in sacred Scripture. The representations of him in the early books are (as it were) barbaric; but as Time advances, nobler views of him are given, Micah and Isaiah transcend Moses, later Psalms (I think he held) became more spiritual; and the Christian doctrine surpasses all. The preacher did not intend any new theory, but pointed at fact. He did not say, nor consciously mean, the earliest books were *not inspired!* yet he virtually said they were not always correct in Theology. Would he (or any other Protestant) say that the *Morality* of the Hebrew books is always *sound?* for in them are grave matters corrected by Jesus himself. I advert to this, because we Protestants seem to have gone beyond Catholics in exalting the Old Testament: as indeed did the Puritans whenever the warlike mood came over them; I must not waste paper and ink on the topic. It increases embarrassment in all controversy, as in the wild outcry against

Bishop Colenso for listening to the objections of a Zulu cattle-driver.

Now, with most friendly and truly sympathetic heart I beg all Protestants who can look tranquilly backward and forward, to see how painfully the *letter* of Scripture has been used against Morality, and has after mischievous stubbornness had to yield. First, as to the evil Calvinism: next, as to Slavery: now, as to the Eternal Hell, which, after darkening awfully the character of God, has grievously intensified the cruelty of man, as in the crusade against Southern France, and the Spanish and Italian Inquisition. The Salvationists have now, I am told, taken up this theory of Divine Cruelty as their main doctrine for frightening dull and lazy souls. Where they convert one thoughtless man they are likely to repel from Christianity ten more thoughtful. Allow to Mr. Davison that the Sacred Letter of the *Old* T. is not perfect; and surely you ought to admit the same of the *New*. This is the Second Reformation now urgently needed; not the fixing of a New Creed, but the unfixing of the arbitrary rule, which forbids the spiritual heart and the merciful heart to move in harmony with advancing literary and scientific knowledge. Resistance to it, if successful, cannot produce a homogeneous Protestant belief, but may (perhaps, must) extend still further the *horrid Paganism* which has so corrupted our educated ranks.

IV. I proceed to a fourth point :. What steps can be taken against the Popish formula of Ordination in the Anglican formularies? I will give my opinion freely, however novel and eccentric it may sound.

The law of England punishes a Gipsy, if, after examining the palm of a housemaid, she elicit *a sixpence* by promising her a young, handsome, and rich husband. I believe an astrologer is similarly punishable for abusing private credulity by any other promise *if he accept money* for his fate-telling First I desire to remark on the condition of getting money by the trade. English law deals only with offences which are on a scale large enough to attract it, and probably thought that diviners who got no money by their divination did not deserve notice. The name of Religion earns many exemptions ; but if that were attempted in England which our press recorded as actual in Mexico some years back, a *lottery of Souls* in which a prize ticket enabled the winner to get one or more of his dead friends more quickly out of Purgatory, our legislators might wake up to suppress it as swindling. In this case they could even point to the money received.

Now, when a man pretends that God has given him power either to forgive sin or to refuse forgiveness, if a credulous votary believe the priest it enslaves him to the priest; and though the priest may not at any stipulated moment exact money payment for the remission of sins, the votary is liable to the demand; and we know that on death-beds there was often great exaction practised. The same principle of law which defends the weak and credulous from the palmistry of gipsies might with equal propriety defend the weak and credulous from the extortion of priests, which indeed may be made at the expense of a dying man's kinsfolk. Some restrictions do exist against clerical terrorism of a dying man, but it is undeniable that the death-bed is not the only place at which enormous power over money can be exercised. If a single M.P. with only one seconder, were to move for a Bill to make it a misdemeanour to pretend to have power or to bestow power of forgiving sin, or refusing forgiveness, his mere motion would force the public to study the question. No new organization, no committees, secretaries, nor public meetings would be requisite. The motion might always be stopt in the Lords, but it would take root in the national heart, and the superstitious formula would be abolished as a swindle early in the twentieth century.

V. The pecuniary funds of the Church are supposed to be the unmanageable difficulty in the case of separating the Churches from the State. I should not have alluded to it, only that all the Puseyites and their successors being here in agreement with the mass of Nonconformists, I desire to renew a protest many times made, that, inasmuch as the Courts of Law enforce deeds and wills of Nonconformists who, with the gift of money, *define a private creed*, the fact *establishes* these sectarians. This never is nor was the practice of churchmen, nor of men of science. If any Nonconformists desire equal and just dealing they ought to claim that no clause of a will or deed defining a creed shall be valid by law, at least (like a copyright) longer than a limited number of years after the date of the will or deed. This would be all on the side of allowing Religious knowledge, like all other knowledge, *to grow up without partial bias,* and thus gravitate into Human and valid knowledge.

PERSECUTION OF HERETICS.

When the Catholics had fallen into ignominy on the Continent, and the Pope was variously insulted by Napoleon the First, their Irish branch still suffered in these islands through our long-enduring memory of past violences. They were then humble and grateful for small mercies. Balked, first by George III., next by the House of Lords, they were encouraged by our Whigs, and (sincerely, I doubt not) renounced Religious Persecution. I have before me the great Catholic Manual (edition 1824) of Milner, which insists that Persecution was never a doctrine of their *Church*, but only a barbarous practice of *Princes* on both sides. The Whigs believed them, and when Emancipation came on in 1829 their renunciation of Persecution helped it through with our statesmen on both sides. But when their object was gained, the Papal policy *cared nothing* for what Irish Catholics had avowed. It had no validity! The Encyclical of Pope Pius the Ninth went into a condemnation of all that since the Peace of Westphalia has been established for general toleration and freedom. In the *Times* and other newspapers it has been observed that of the converts to Rome in this century not one dares to condemn Persecution of Heretics. My brother is an eminent case, for he wrote to the London *Times* that, though to *see* a Spanish *auto da fé* he believes would kill him, he cannot condemn it ecclesiastically. It may seem that just because Englishmen love freedom, the converts are jealously examined by their Directors as to the soundness of their faith about killing and punishing heretics.

It so happened that among the very few interchanges of opinion that for sixty-six years I had with my brother, one was on this very matter, Persecution of Heretics. Perhaps I had said: " To me the historic fact of the Roman-Church persecution, with her *justification* of it, is a sufficient confutation of her lofty pretensions." I soon gave up argument, because I thought that futile. I will add here what I would have said if I had not thought him a *poisoned mind*, which dared not think for itself upon the topic.

He knew, and every half-educated man knows, that morality is older than any known National Religion; that many Established and National Religions have been *immoral*—among other immoralities have had murderous sacrifices and foul use of women. Hebrew prophets and Christian teachers have always held it as an *Axiom* that to point at *immorality* imbedded in a Pagan rite was a sufficient confutation. Of course the immorality must not be interpreted by any one nation, but by collective humanity, which, as Hesiod and Aristotle say, is a voice of God. When Paul exhorts the Philippians to follow whatsoever things are just, pure, lovely, and of good report, he appeals, not to anything sectarian, but to the Universal Conscience. This it is, of good report, that brings Paganism before its tribunal, and sometimes condemns it. Every form of Christianity which offends this higher law is *ipso facto* refuted and untenable.

If Christians of the first or second century

had avowed their intention to set up what *we now know* as the Spanish Inquisition, *as soon as they were able*,—any energetic Roman Emperor might have massacred them, as we have hanged Thugs, to extirpate *the execrable superstition*, and the nations everywhere would have shouted " Well done ! It was right to strike before they could ripen their aims into deeds." Happily, no thought of murdering those who did not believe him, has ever been attributed to *Jesus:* everything from him is to the opposite tendency. Those who pretend to be his disciples, whether in Rome or Russia or Abyssinia, who use force under pretence of Christianity, condemn their system as *Un-*Christian and worse than Noble Paganism.

But I proceed to tell how my brother defended the Persecution of those who will not give to fellow-mortals the allegiance which their conscience commands to God only. In " the ages of faith," says he, the populace everywhere saw that Heresy (that is, Disobedience to Holy Church) was a crime on the same scale as murder or high treason; then the Church was able to call on the Civil Power to inflict the just doom. As men become more enlightened the same state of the public conscience *may recur.* Over the width of the Continents the millions may recognize the crime of refusing allegiance to the Church, just as the crime of Revolt against the State. With Collective Humanity sanctioning her cry for Vengeance the Church will then be *able* to punish Disobedience. She cannot now; therefore at present the attempt would be a mistake. But you have no right to assume that what was the wide-world morality at a time to which we can point in the ages of faith, will not return. Then the Church will judge for herself what is expedient and what is necessary.

The reader will at once see how clear was his argument and how easy to remember; though of course I pledge myself only to the substance. It called to my memory an anecdote current in Oxford (perhaps in 1837) concerning a talk between J. H. N. and his disciple X. Y. The latter, rubbing his hands with glee, says, "Dear, dear Mr. N., when shall WE begin to persecute?" Mr. N. playfully rubs his hands in imitation, and replies, "My dear fellow, *as soon as we are* ABLE."

This seemed to me a cleverly-made-up joke, which deserved only a laugh. But on hearing my brother's own defence of Persecution (perhaps constructed only because, being enslaved, he must say *something* for the abomination), the argument is very fairly summed up in the words, " As soon as we are *able*, we (that is, Roman Policy) *will* persecute."

I do not write as an alarmist. The educator is abroad wherever the Locomotive and Press can reach. I do not believe in the recurrence of dire barbarism. But a Power that *wishes* to imprison or kill, and cannot, will use mean tricks such as baptizing a Jewish child and then claiming him as a Christian. There is nothing too little for its mean spite, or too large for its ambition. Protestants ought never to harbour an unkind thought against a *private* Catholic as such; yet never to forget that, where private judgment is forbidden, no man's conscience is in his own keeping.

My last word to Protestants is to say plainly *why* I have undertaken this very painful task. A great effort seems to have been made to prepare currency in the book-market for works written by my brother when he was in the Anglican Church fifty years ago. The present generation seems not to know that his teaching, since 1833 at least, swept his peculiar disciples sideways towards Rome; the fact attests these works to be of Romish tendency. The "Apologia" has been trumpeted as a victorious proof that, while an Anglican, he had *no* Romanist tendency. I read a few days back in a popular print ridicule of "a few *old-fashioned* parsons" who believed that J. H. Newman was *at heart* a Romanist *while ostensibly an Anglican*. It does not seem to occur to some people that "*old-fashioned*" means elder—that elder men can remember things sixty and more years old, of which the later generation knows nothing soundly. I protest that *in honesty* any edition of my brother's writing while he was a *nominal* Anglican ought to state in the *title* page, or some equally conspicuous place, that he was *already* a hater of the Reformation, and eager to convert us to Romanism. My brother hated Protestantism, and accepted as a divine mission to supplant it (I do not say by Popery, but) by full Romanism. As warning to incautious parents, I have felt it my duty to exhibit the facts.

Scholars like my very able friend Dr. James Martineau may read with profit my brother's works; so perhaps may Mr. Richard Hutton. But parents who would be sorely grieved by their children becoming converts to Romanism will not be wise in exposing the young and inexperienced to the speciousness of his pleadings.

F. W. N.

www.ingramcontent.com/pod-product-compliance
Lightning Source LLC
Chambersburg PA
CBHW030343170426
43202CB00010B/1228